It's another great book from CGP...

This book is for anyone doing **GCSE Edexcel Religious Studies, Units 1-5: Religion and Life**.

It covers all the important information and issues in a **clear** and **balanced** way, with plenty of advice for writing **top-notch answers** in the exam. There's even a section to help you score full marks for your **spelling**, **punctuation** and **grammar**.

What's more, we've included a **free** Online Edition of the whole book, so you can revise on a computer or tablet — wherever you are.

How to get your free Online Edition

Just go to **cgpbooks.co.uk/extras** and enter this code...

2903 1458 4963 9564

By the way, this code only works for one person. If somebody else has used this book before you, they might have already claimed the Online Edition.

CGP — still the best! ☺

Our sole aim here at CGP is to produce the highest quality books — carefully written, immaculately presented and dangerously close to being funny.

Then we work our socks off to get them out to you — at the cheapest possible prices.

Contents

Section Four — Religion and Community Cohesion

Guide to Symbols

This book covers Religion and Life Based on a Study of **Christianity** (including Roman Catholic Christianity), **Islam** and **Judaism**.
The clouds in the corners of the pages tell you whether the page covers:

the **Christian** view...

...the **Muslim** view...

...the **Jewish** view...

...or general views that **everyone** doing a Religion and Life unit needs to learn.

Bible / Qur'an References

References from the Bible always go in the order: ***Book Chapter:Verse(s)***.
So whenever you see something like: ***Mark 3:5-6***, it means it's from the book of Mark, Chapter 3, Verses 5-6.

Similarly, references from the Qur'an are shown with the ***Surah (Chapter)*** followed by the ***Ayat (Verse)***.

Published by CGP

Editors:
Sharon Keeley, Luke von Kotze, Andy Park, Jo Sharrock, Julie Wakeling

Contributors:
Maria Amayuelas-Tann, Jill Hudson, Paul D. Smith

ISBN: 978 1 84762 301 0

With thanks to Mary Falkner for the proofreading.
With thanks to Laura Jakubowski for the copyright research.

Groovy website: www.cgpbooks.co.uk

Jolly bits of clipart from CorelDRAW®
Printed by Elanders Ltd, Newcastle upon Tyne

Based on the classic CGP style created by Richard Parsons.

Your Opinions Matter

General

Welcome to Religious Studies — it may be a little bit different from the subjects you've studied before. This book covers half of the full course GCSE, or the whole of the short course GCSE. You get lots of options for RS, so make sure you've got the right book before you start.

In RS you get Marks for More than just Knowledge

In GCSE Religious Studies there are two 'assessment objectives' — these are the skills you'll need to show to get marks in the exams. You get half your marks for each.

1) The first gives you marks for describing and explaining what you know.
2) The second gives you marks for making arguments backed up with well-thought-out reasoning — and for understanding and explaining other people's opinions.

What You Think Matters...

1) So unlike most of the other subjects you might have exams on (such as maths), in RS you're supposed to think about what you're learning and come to your own conclusions.
2) A lot of the topics you study are pretty controversial — such as euthanasia. In RS you have to decide where you stand on these difficult issues.
3) In fact, being able to give reasoned opinions will count for half your marks.

In my opinion — that is an awesome hat.

...But You've Still Got a Lot to Learn

1) Unfortunately, you can't just weigh in with opinions based on how you feel that afternoon. In the exam you have to back up what you say with reasons. Those reasons will be what you've learnt during the course.
2) You'll also need to know the reasons why some people might disagree with you. In other words, you'll have to present both sides of an argument.
3) And don't forget, the other half of your marks comes from just knowing things. As much as you need to be able to argue, you'll still need to learn all the basics — what things mean and what different people believe.

There'll be Fact Questions and Opinion Questions

So in the exam you'll get questions like:

What is omni-benevolence?

For these you have to give the definitions of the words you've learnt. There's a glossary in the back that should help you learn them.

As well as questions like:

Do you think miracles prove that God exists? Give two reasons for your point of view.

For which you'll need to give your own opinion — backed up with reasons.

And some like:

Choose one religion and explain its teachings on divorce.

For these you'll need to give details about the religion(s) you've studied.

And some questions will ask you to: Give reasons why some people may disagree with you.

This means for each topic you're going to have to:

1) Learn the facts.
2) Work out what you think and why.
3) Learn why people might disagree with you.

What do you think of it so far?

It turns out that you have to do twice as much as you might have thought. First you've got to commit each topic to memory, and then you have to figure out what your take on it is. I guess in some ways it's unavoidable, given that this course is about what people believe. And I believe it's about time for some Religious Studies — oh yes.

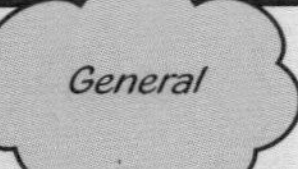

A Religious Upbringing

Millions of people across the world believe in some kind of divine being or 'god'.
They believe for various reasons — for some people, it's based on personal religious experience, but for others it's more indirect. For many people, the fact that they're brought up in a religious environment leads to or supports belief in a god.

Religious Belief Can Start with Your Upbringing

1) Children generally believe what their parents tell them, and tend to copy their parents' behaviour.
2) So, if a child is brought up by religious parents, with an upbringing that's based on religious teaching, it's more likely that they'll believe in a god.
3) For example, most Christian parents will have their children baptised soon after they're born, take them to pray in church, send them to Sunday school to learn about the Christian faith and encourage them to be confirmed as Christians when they're old enough. They'll also take part in religious festivals, e.g. performing in a nativity play at Christmas.
   At home, church and Sunday school, there are trusted adults who set an example of belief in God, and can help a child to develop their own faith.
4) The same would apply if you grew up in a religious community or went to a religious school (e.g. a Roman Catholic school, a Jewish Cheder or a Muslim Madrasah) where life is based on faith in one particular religion.
5) Different religions have different attitudes towards raising children in their faith:

CHRISTIANITY

1) According to the New Testament, you cannot be 'born a Christian'.
2) It's said that God has no grandchildren. In other words, you can't rely on your parents' faith — you have to find your own. And your parents can't force you to accept Christianity — it's your decision.

Evangelical Christians in particular stress this — and they use various expressions to describe it, such as 'being born again', 'being converted', etc.

I'm a Jew.
I'm a Muslim.
Um... I'll think about it later...

JUDAISM

1) Jews believe that if your mother is Jewish, you're Jewish — whether you like it or not.
2) However, practising Jews recognise the importance of encouraging their children to 'keep the faith'.

ISLAM

1) Muslims believe that everyone is born in submission to Allah.
2) They may walk away from Allah as a result of their upbringing, but this is not the way things were meant to be.
3) If someone embraces Islam later in life, he or she is said to be 'returning'.

Christians, Muslims and Jews have Similar Beliefs about God

Since Christianity and Islam both developed from Judaism, the basic concept of God (the Christian God, the Muslim Allah or the Jewish Almighty) is something that all three faiths share. God is believed to be:

OMNIPOTENT: all-powerful — nothing is impossible for God.

OMNISCIENT: all-knowing — knowing everything that we do, think or feel, now, in the past and in the future.

OMNI-BENEVOLENT: all-loving and all-compassionate — he wants only what's best for us.

The nature of God — well I thought I'd ease you in gently...

So despite their differences, it seems Christians, Jews and Muslims all agree on the fundamentals — that God/Allah is supreme, all-powerful, all-knowing and compassionate. So far, so good. Read on...

Religious Experiences

General

There are loads of ways people claim to experience God.
For believers, these religious experiences allow people to 'know' God as he reveals himself to them.

Religious Experiences May Lead to Belief in a God

God can reveal his presence in different ways...

1) NUMINOUS
This describes an experience that inspires awe and wonder, where someone can feel God's presence. For example, a beautiful view or a butterfly's wing might convince you there must be a creator.

2) MIRACLES
Miracles are amazing events that can't be explained by the laws of nature or science. The Bible is full of accounts of Jesus's miracles. People claim miracles still occur (miracles of healing at Lourdes, for example) and bring people to God.
Miracles are said to show God's power and presence.

Nothing up my sleeves...

3) PRAYER
Prayer is an attempt to contact God directly. It usually involves words and can be thought of as a conversation with God. A person might feel the presence of God in an answered prayer e.g. if an ill person they pray for is cured, or they are filled with a sense of inner peace or wonder.

4) RELIGIOUS SCRIPTURE
People can read religious scripture (e.g. the Bible, the Qur'an or the Torah), and feel that the nature of God has been revealed.

5) CHARISMATIC PHENOMENA (or Charismatic Worship)
Following conversion, a Christian believer may claim to have been "touched by the Holy Spirit" and begin 'speaking in tongues' (unknown languages), having visions or prophesying (speaking a message from God). They may also sing, dance, shake or cry during worship.

Conversion refers to the first time a person becomes a follower of a god (although it can also be used when someone changes their faith). They might say they've been 'saved' or 'born again'.

BUT THERE ARE PLENTY OF SCEPTICS AROUND...

A key concern for nonbelievers is whether the experiences are real.

Sceptics argue that they're just illusions brought on by religious hysteria or a desire to believe in something. Or that events that seem miraculous can actually be explained by science.

Revelation can be General (for Everyone) or Special (a Personal Visit)

General revelation refers to experiences which are available to everyone, including:

1) acts of nature, conscience and morality,
2) religious scripture,
3) the work of religious leaders.

Special revelation describes experiences of God revealing himself directly to an individual or to a select group, e.g.:

1) visions,
2) dreams,
3) prophecies.

"I've got a revelation here for a Mr Smith..."

Revelations, eh... Wow. I mean, just imagine. It's just mind-blowing...

General

Design and Causation

There are two main philosophical arguments for the existence of a god.
These are usually referred to as the argument from design and the argument from causation.

Design: "Someone Must Have Designed the Universe"

1) Many people are convinced of the existence of a god by 'design' arguments.
2) The idea here is that the intricate workings of the Universe (or of life) can't have come about by random chance. There must have been some kind of designer — and this designer was God.
3) Isaac Newton's thumb theory (because every thumbprint is intricate and unique, there must be a God) and William Paley's watchmaker theory (you wouldn't think an intricate watch you found was made by chance — so why believe the world was) are both design arguments.
4) Even Albert Einstein, one of the most prominent scientists of the twentieth century (and an agnostic — see below), said: "When I see all the glories of the cosmos, I can't help but believe that there is a divine hand behind it all."
5) Einstein might have been talking about design, but this might also be interpreted as a reference to a 'numinous' experience — something which inspires awe and wonder at God's creation (see page 3).

Causation: "There Must Have Been a First Cause"

1) The Universe as we know it works on the principle of 'cause and effect' — that is, everything that happens is caused by something else.
2) So an event happening now was caused by an earlier event, which in turn was caused by an even earlier event and so on back through time.
3) If you trace this chain of cause and effect back in time, you find two possibilities:

> a) The chain goes back forever — i.e. the Universe has always existed, it's eternal.
> b) You eventually reach a starting point — an uncaused cause or 'First Cause'.

4) Some people argue that this 'First Cause' must have been God.

But Not Everyone is Convinced by these Arguments

1) These philosophical arguments convince many people of the existence of God.

2) However, non-religious ideas about the origin of the world might lead a person to become an agnostic (someone who doesn't know whether or not there's a god — strictly, someone who believes it's impossible to know whether there's a god or not) or an atheist (someone who rejects completely the idea of a divine being).
3) These ideas include the theory of evolution (often called Darwinism) and the Big Bang theory (cosmology) (more about those on the next page).
4) Cosmologists argue that the Big Bang theory offers an alternative 'First Cause'. According to the theory, both space and time started with the Big Bang. If this is true, then to ask what came 'before' the Big Bang or what 'caused' the Big Bang is meaningless.

Looks like the jury's still out on this one...

Philosophers have been arguing backwards and forwards about this sort of thing for thousands of years. But religion's a personal thing — Sam gazes at the stars and reckons there must be a god but Al doesn't believe at all. Whichever side you're on, you need to learn these reasons for believing (or not) for your exam.

The Origins of the World

Christianity, Islam, Judaism & General

No one saw exactly how the Earth came to be like it is... but science and religion both have their theories.

Scientific Arguments — There are Two Main Types

COSMOLOGICAL THEORIES — How the Universe came into being

Chief amongst these is the Big Bang theory. It says that the Universe began in an explosion of matter and energy. Matter from this explosion eventually formed stars, planets and everything else. The Universe still seems to be expanding today — important evidence for this theory.

EVOLUTIONARY THEORIES — How living things came to be like they are today

In 1859, Charles Darwin published 'On the Origin of the Species'. In this book he argued that all life on the planet originated from simple cells. Life evolved over millions of years into a huge variety of forms. According to this theory, we evolved from apes — not from Adam and Eve.

These theories are at odds with many religious arguments. However, if you don't take everything in the Bible or Torah literally, scientific and religious ideas can exist in harmony. Science tells us how, religion tells us why.

Religions have their Own Ideas about all this...

Christian Ideas

1) Christian and Jewish ideas about Creation come from the same scriptures, and so are quite similar.
2) Christian thinking is based on the idea that God created everything. If the Bible is taken literally the process took six days, and humankind didn't evolve from apes but is descended from Adam and Eve.
3) However, it can also be viewed as a parable, or as a symbolic description of a more gradual evolution. This means it's possible to believe in the Bible and science.
4) In 1996 the Roman Catholic Church accepted the Big Bang theory — definitely a significant acceptance of science.

For example, the Bible says things were created in the following order — the heavens (i.e. space) and Earth, the atmosphere, land and sea, and then plants, animals and people. This is pretty much the same order as scientists believe things appeared. So the timescale is different (millions of years rather than six days), but the general idea is the same.

"In the beginning God created the heavens and the earth." Genesis 1:1 NIV

Yeah, not bad. I reckon I deserve a day off.

Jewish Ideas

1) Orthodox Jews, who see the Torah as the word of God and so literally true, would find it difficult to accept scientific arguments about creation. God is believed to have created the world in six days. And humanity is believed to have started with Adam and Eve.
2) Reform Jews might argue that Creation as described in the Torah is more a way for us to understand, not an explanation of how it happened.

Islamic Ideas

1) Muslims believe that Allah created the world and everything in it.
2) However, unlike Christianity and Judaism, descriptions of creation in the Qur'an are not entirely at odds with science. Islam does not really compete with the Big Bang theory or Darwinism. In fact, scientific theories are supported by passages such as this.

"Have those who disbelieved not considered that the heavens and the earth were a joined entity, and We separated them and made from water every living thing? Then will they not believe?" Qur'an 21:30

In the beginning, God created Exams...

Albert Einstein once said that if you see something beautiful or amazing, you are seeing the work of God. Yeah, well... what did thicky Einstein know... But whether the Universe came to be this way through chance or design is a key question in the science versus religion debate. (More about that on the previous page.)

Evil and Suffering

Loads of bad things happen in the world. People suffer from terrible illnesses and die in pain. Some people commit horrible crimes and other people suffer as a result. These issues often cause people to ask why. For religious people, the bigger question is: "Why is God letting this happen?"

Evil can be Either Human-Made or Natural

Evil and suffering can be divided into two types:

MORAL (HUMAN-MADE) EVIL

1) This is when suffering is brought about by the cruel actions of people.
2) This includes things like murder, war, rape and torture.
3) The person causing the evil is able to make a choice about what is morally right or wrong.

NATURAL EVIL

1) This kind of evil, and the suffering that comes with it, is caused by the world in which we live, and is no-one's 'fault'.
2) This includes things like disease, floods, earthquakes and hurricanes.
3) However, many recent natural disasters may have been caused by human interference in the natural world, raising the question of whether that makes those events human-made.

Evil can Lead People to Question their Faith

1) Evil and suffering may lead some people to question their belief in God — or even to reject their faith.
2) This might be because they can't believe that a God who is good would allow such things to happen, or because they feel that their prayers are not being answered (i.e. they think God could help, but doesn't).

UNANSWERED PRAYERS

Roman Catholics and Orthodox Christians often pray for a saint to intercede with God on behalf of someone who's suffering. These are called 'intercessory prayers'. In other Christian traditions, prayers of intercession for others are addressed directly to God. As are prayers for help in Judaism and Islam (called du'a in Islam).

Christianity, Judaism and Islam teach that no sincere prayer goes unheard or unanswered.

And that if a prayer seems to be unanswered, it's just that we can't understand God's reply. Since no human can ever know God's plan, it's impossible to say what's really best for us.

Praying for and helping those who suffer is often seen as a key part of various faiths.

3) Other people might argue that God can't be very powerful if he is unable to prevent suffering (i.e. God can't help, even if he wanted to).

The Christian View — Adam & Eve, a Test of Faith...

1) Christianity and Judaism teach that evil entered the world as a result of Adam and Eve giving in to temptation in the Garden of Eden — this switch from a perfect world to one containing evil is known as 'The Fall'.
2) After the Fall, every human being was born with a flawed nature, capable of causing suffering — this is the idea of original sin.
3) Christians believe God created humans with free will — it's up to us to choose whether we perform evil deeds or not — just as it was up to Adam and Eve whether to give in to temptation or not.

oops...

Christianity and Judaism differ in that Christians believe Jesus was put on Earth to pay for the sins of all humankind.

4) Suffering is often seen as a test of faith — God has his reasons (even if we don't know what they are). Christians believe that they should try to help people who are suffering — both practically and by praying.

Not the cheeriest page in the book, for sure...

Eeek — we're into evil and suffering already. Many people have tried to work out what exactly evil is. Some argue that human-made evil is a psychological disorder that some people are more prone to than others.

Evil and Suffering

Islam & Judaism

The problem of evil, why people suffer, and how to deal with it. It's the sort of thing religion was invented for.

Islam and Judaism also say we have the Choice...

1) Both Islam and Judaism teach that humankind was created with free will.
2) Therefore, people can choose to follow God, or choose to do wrong.
3) Islam and Judaism also have similar perspectives on how to deal with suffering and evil.

Judaism says Suffering can have Positive Results

1) The Book of Job in the Hebrew Bible contains a key Jewish idea on evil and suffering. Job endures terrible suffering of all kinds and he questions God. In the end Job comes to the conclusion that God is all-powerful and knows what he is doing — and that suffering must be accepted because we can't really understand the world or God's plan.
2) Judaism teaches that we have free will and are able to choose what we do (like Adam and Eve — see page 6). But we are prone to making mistakes, which could lead to suffering.
3) Like many Christians, Jews may also respond to suffering and evil through prayer.
4) The Jewish approach to suffering often stresses the idea that good can come out of terrible suffering. Suffering can bring people closer to each other and closer to God. It also allows people to make sacrifices for other people and draw on their inner strength.
5) The following passage is taken from the Midrash (a collection of Rabbinical commentaries on the Tenakh or Jewish Bible): "Not to have known suffering is not to be truly human." It suggests that suffering is simply a part of the human experience and, therefore, must be accepted.

Bet you a fiver he'll crack...

Although Satan isn't a part of modern Judaism, he does give Job a hard time.

The Qur'an says "We Will Surely Test You"

1) Muslims believe that evil is a test of humanity's free will. We have free will so can choose whether to give in to temptation or not. It's a test of faith.
2) Islam teaches that if we choose to act against the will of Allah we will have to answer for that wrongdoing on the Day of Judgement.
3) The following passage is taken from the Qur'an 2:155-156:

> "And We will surely test you with something of fear and hunger and a loss of wealth and lives and fruits, but give good tidings to the patient, who, when disaster strikes them, say, 'Indeed we belong to Allah, and indeed to Him we will return.' "

This is remarkably similar to the moral of the Book of Job, when you think about it.

4) The idea here is that suffering should be accepted. Muslims believe that, despite suffering in this life, there will be joy in the next as Allah is compassionate.
5) Prayer is one way of coping with evil and suffering. If people pray for forgiveness when they have done wrong they will be forgiven. One of the ninety-nine revealed names of Allah is Al-Ghaffar — The Forgiver.
6) Muslims believe that those who are suffering should be treated compassionately by others. Many Muslims work to help those who are suffering.

There are differences in belief and tradition within Judaism and Islam, as there are within all religions.

"Will I be forgiven?" — "Best ask the Ghaffar"...

Christianity, Judaism and Islam all have pretty similar ideas about this stuff: 1) Suffering is often seen as a test of faith. 2) You should always try to help others who are suffering. 3) Evil is wrong, but if you pray for forgiveness after doing something wrong, God/Allah will be merciful and will forgive you.

Christianity, Islam, Judaism & General

The Media: Belief

TV programmes, radio programmes and films can have a big impact on people's beliefs.

A Christian Example: "Songs of Praise"

The majority of TV programmes are non-religious, but there are a few dedicated religious programmes around that might affect people's attitudes to belief in God. One of the best-known is the BBC's "Songs of Praise", which features Christian hymns and focuses on a different community or theme each week.

SONGS OF PRAISE — SUNDAY EVENINGS, BBC 1

Positive effects on faith:

1) Viewers share other people's experiences of God and faith. This can help show the relevance of Christianity to people's lives, and make them feel part of a larger community.
2) The themes covered in the programme can lead to a deeper understanding of the Christian religion.
3) The programme is interactive — with hymn and prayer text on screen. This lets viewers take part in communal worship without having to go to church.

Negative effects on faith:

1) It's hard to feel personally involved in a service when you're watching it on TV.
2) The programme might be seen to trivialise the act of worship.
3) Some people find the traditional hymns boring and uninspiring.

BBC Radio 4 also broadcasts religious programmes, including "Sunday Worship" at 8:10 a.m.

Judaism is Sometimes Stereotyped by the Media

1) You don't tend to get regular, specifically Jewish programmes on national TV or radio, and this is a cause for some concern and frustration in the Jewish community.
2) Many feel that Jewish issues are not always dealt with fairly and that Jews are shown in a stereotypical way (e.g. passive victims in Holocaust films like "Schindler's List", neurotic intellectuals in Woody Allen films like "Annie Hall" or pushy, overprotective mothers in US sit-coms like "Will and Grace").

But in June 2008, BBC 4 broadcast an in-depth series of programmes called "Jews" that looked at the history, religious practices and beliefs of different groups of Jews in Britain today. Programmes like this may help Jews to reconnect with their faith, as well as educating the non-Jewish community.

Islam has Been in the Spotlight Since 9/11

Since the rise of Islamic fundamentalism, Islam and its link with terrorism have been all over the news.

Programmes like Channel 4's "Qur'an" (first shown in July 2008) have tried to show a more balanced view of Islam. "Qur'an" looked at how different groups of people interpret the sacred text differently.

Some Other Muslim Programming:

- "Devotional Sounds: Islam" on BBC's Asian Network radio station broadcasts religious music every Saturday and Sunday morning.
- Muslim clerics regularly contribute to Radio 4's "Thought for the Day".

An Atheist Viewpoint: "The Root of All Evil?"

1) Atheist programmes and literature might lead people to question the existence of God.
2) In January 2006, Channel 4 showed a two-part series by atheist Professor Richard Dawkins called "The Root of All Evil?" related to his book "The God Delusion".
3) In these programmes, he argued that what he called 'a process of non-thinking called faith' has led to intolerance, violence and destruction whilst preaching peace and brotherhood.

I've told you before — The Simpsons™ is NOT a religion...

These are just examples, though, so don't worry if they're not the ones you've studied. You need to know how two TV or radio shows or films might affect someone's attitudes to faith and belief in God.

Practice Questions

Makes you think doesn't it... Is there a God? Why is there suffering in the world? Who actually watches Songs of Praise?
You need to have your own views on this stuff, but you won't get far in the exam if you don't know some religious teachings as well. So try these questions, and if there are any you can't answer, go back and have another look at the section. Then try the questions again until you can do them all.
(If you're struggling with the wordy questions, check out the exam help pages at the back of the book.)
In the exam, your spelling, punctuation and grammar will be assessed in your answers to this section — there are 4 extra marks up for grabs, so make sure your writing is accurate (see p.41-44).

1) What is:
   a) omnipotence?
   b) omniscience?
   c) omni-benevolence?
   d) conversion?
   e) a numinous experience?
   f) atheism?
   g) agnosticism?
   h) moral evil?
   i) free will?

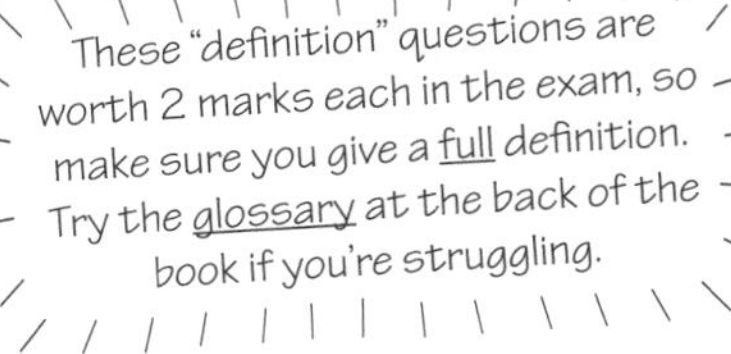

These "definition" questions are worth 2 marks each in the exam, so make sure you give a full definition. Try the glossary at the back of the book if you're struggling.

2) For each of the following questions, give two reasons for your point of view.
   a) Do you think miracles show the presence of God?
   b) Do you think religious experiences are real?
   c) Do you think God designed the Universe?
   d) Do you believe good can come from suffering?
   e) Do religious programmes on the TV make people more likely to believe in God?

These questions are asking for your opinion as well as reasons to back it up. These questions are worth 4 marks each, so you have to give detailed reasons.

3) For these questions, you need to express yourself as clearly as possible — make sure your writing is correct, accurate and well organised.
   a) Explain how a religious upbringing might lead to a belief in God.
   b) Choose one religious experience and explain how it might lead to a belief in God.
   c) Choose one religion and explain how its followers respond to scientific theories about the origin of the world.
   d) Choose one religion and explain how its followers respond to the problem of unanswered prayers.
   e) Choose two television programmes, radio programmes or films and explain how they might affect a person's belief in God.

"Explain" means you have to say why, not just what people believe. These questions test your 'clarity of expression' as well as what you know. They're worth 8 marks each in the exam, so they're important.

4) Read the following statements:
   a) "The Universe had to be caused by God."
   b) "God created the Universe and everything in it in six days."
   c) "The presence of evil and suffering in the world shows that there is no God."
   d) "Evil is a test of our free will."

   For each statement:
   (i) Do you agree? Give reasons for your opinion.
   (ii) Give reasons why some people may disagree with you.
   In your answers you should refer to at least one religion.

More opinion questions — worth 3 marks for each side of the argument. But this time, you have to give some religious views in your answer. If you don't refer to a religion in at least one part of the question you lose half the marks, straight off.

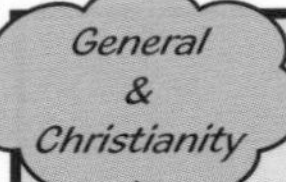
General
&
Christianity

Life After Death: Christianity

What people believe will happen to them after death can influence the way they live their lives.

Life After Death — Some People Believe, Others Don't

1) Some people believe that when you die, that's it — your body decays and you cease to exist.
2) Others believe that, although your body may die and decay, your soul can live on — in other words, you move on to a different kind of existence. This is the basic idea of life after death.

Near-Death Experiences and the Paranormal

There are many reasons why people believe (or don't believe) in life after death.

1) Most religions teach that we all move on to an afterlife of some kind. For some people, this will be enough to make them believe in life after death — they have faith in what their religion teaches.
2) Other people use near-death experiences to argue that a soul exists after death. A near-death experience usually involves an out-of-body experience when someone is close to death. While apparently physically dead, they glimpse what they believe to be an afterlife, or speak to long-dead family members.
3) Not everyone believes that these visions are real though. They argue that hallucinations could be a result of chemical activity in the brain when it's short of oxygen.

I believe science can explain the paranormal.

4) The paranormal (things science can't explain, which are thought to have a spiritual cause, e.g. ghosts) is sometimes used as evidence of life after death. Some people (mediums) claim they can talk to the dead.
5) Other people reckon these events have a scientific explanation — maybe we don't know what the explanation is yet, but there will be one. And some people don't believe these events happen in the first place.
6) Some people claim to have evidence of reincarnation (having lived a previous life, died and been reborn in a new body). Lots of research has been carried out with young children who claim to remember past lives, and the evidence has some people convinced. But sceptics suggest that the memories aren't real — that they must have been suggested to the children in some way.

Christian Teaching — Heaven and Hell

1) Christianity teaches that the soul lives on after death (immortality of the soul), and that the body will be resurrected (brought back to life) for Judgement Day, just as Jesus was resurrected after his crucifixion.
2) Christians believe that God will judge you, and you'll go either to Heaven, or to Hell:
   - Heaven is often portrayed as a place of great beauty and serenity, a paradise where you'll spend eternity with God — as long as you believe in Jesus Christ, have followed his teachings and have lived a good life, that is. Those in Heaven are said to belong to the Communion of Saints.
   - Hell, on the other hand, is portrayed as a place of torment and pain — the final destination of nonbelievers and those who have led bad lives.
3) However, not all Christians believe that these are real places — many Christians see Heaven and Hell as states of mind. In Heaven you'll be happy, and know God — in Hell you'll be unable to know God's love.
4) A few believe that those who God finds unacceptable will be annihilated. They had no interest in spiritual things when they were alive, therefore their spirits were never awakened and cannot survive death.
5) Roman Catholics also believe in a place, or state of existence, called Purgatory. Here sins are punished before the soul is able to move on to Heaven. This concept isn't in the Bible, so Protestants reject it.
6) The fear of punishment or promise of rewards in the afterlife encourages believers to live good lives. But many Christians believe even those who led sinful lives may find salvation thanks to God's saving power.

And in Hell they make you wear bad wigs and false moustaches... forever.

Get ready to do some soul searching...

I wonder if we're all destined to an afterlife of moving people's car keys and eating socks? Mmm... socks...

Life After Death: Islam

Islam

Islam, like other religions, has very definite teachings when it comes to life after death.

Akhirah — Life After Death

1) Muslims call life after death akhirah — it's one of the key Islamic beliefs. Not to have a belief in life after death would make this life meaningless for a Muslim.

Only Allah knows why he tests us in these ways.

2) Islam teaches that nothing that happens to us during our earthly lives is accidental — Muslims believe we are being tested, and that the way we act in life will determine what happens to us after we die.
3) A key teaching of Islam is that we remain in the grave after death in a state called barzakh (the cold sleep) until the Day of Judgement. On this day, Allah will judge everyone — not just Muslims.

The Soul Goes to al'Jannah (Paradise) or Jahannam (Hell)

1) Although the earthly life is short compared with the eternal, Muslims believe it's still very important. It's in this life that Allah tests us. On Judgement Day, it's too late to beg forgiveness for any wrongdoing.
2) Islam teaches we are judged on:
   i) our character,
   ii) our reactions to good and bad events in life,
   iii) our way of life.
3) Muslims believe everything is the will of Allah — so there's no point moaning about your circumstances. We cannot know why things happen, or what Allah wishes us to learn from it. The important thing is that we react to it the right way.
4) The reward for those who have followed Allah will be entry into al'Jannah (Paradise) — this is a place of peace, happiness and beauty. In fact, the Qur'an refers to al'Jannah as 'gardens of delight', filled with flowers and birdsong.
5) For those who don't believe in Allah, or have committed bad deeds, the reward is Jahannam (or Hell). The Qur'an describes Jahannam as a place of scorching fire, hot winds and black smoke. Here, those who have ignored Allah's teaching and failed to act righteously will be punished for eternity.
6) But Allah is also merciful, so many of those who have lived sinful lives may not be sent to Jahannam.

Allah is merciful and compassionate, but at the same time, he's a tough judge. Basically, if you're a good Muslim, you'll go to Paradise. But if you're a bad Muslim or a non-Muslim, you deserve Hell, but you might get lucky and be sent by Allah to Paradise if he's feeling merciful.

The Soul is the Real Person

1) Muslims believe human beings are Allah's greatest physical creation. They also believe that humans are different from other animals, because we know we will die.
2) Islam teaches that every soul (ruh) is unique and has free will.
3) On Judgement Day, it is the soul that will be resurrected and judged, as it is the soul that is our consciousness. Our body is thought of as a kind of 'vehicle for the soul'.

It's free will that makes human beings different from angels — angels obey Allah perfectly.

Muslims believe in predestination — Al-Qadr. Although we have free will, Islam teaches we cannot do everything we want — God is still in control. In recognition of this, Muslims will often say "insh' Allah" (if God is willing).

Stop moaning about your Exam — it is the will of Allah...

Don't be put off by the long and difficult words on this page — just get learning and your RS exam will fly by. Don't worry, there's only another eight pages to go in this section... (...what did I say about the moaning...)

Judaism

Life After Death: Judaism

It should come as no surprise at all to learn that Judaism has something to say about death as well.

Sheol — the Shadowy Destination of the Dead

1) Jewish teachings are largely concerned with the earthly life, and a person's duties to God and other people. According to the Torah, rewards for obeying God and punishments for 'breaking the covenant' are sent in this world.
2) But Jews still have a firm belief in the immortality of the soul.
3) When the earliest Jewish scriptures were written, it was believed that after death all souls went to a place called Sheol — where the dead lived as shadows. Sheol was believed to be dark and cold, and your soul would stay there for eternity. This wasn't as a punishment — it's just what was believed to happen.
4) However, over time the Jews came to believe in the resurrection of the dead...

"If you follow my decrees... I will send you rain in its season, and the ground will yield its crops and the trees of the field their fruit... and you will eat all the food you want and live in safety in your land. I will grant peace in the land, and you will lie down and no one will make you afraid... and I will keep my covenant with you.

But if you will not listen to me... and abhor my laws... and so violate my covenant... I will bring upon you sudden terror, wasting diseases and fever that will destroy your sight and drain away your life. You will plant seed in vain... I will set my face against you... those who hate you will rule over you..." Leviticus 26:3-17 NIV

In the Messianic Age the Dead Will be Resurrected

1) Jews believe that the Messiah, a great future leader, will bring an era of perfect peace and prosperity called the World to Come (or messianic age). (Jews don't believe Jesus was the Messiah.)
2) It's believed that the righteous dead (both Jews and non-Jews) will be resurrected to share in the messianic peace. But the wicked dead won't be resurrected — they gave up their share in the World to Come by living sinful lives.

"Multitudes who sleep in the dust of the earth will awake: some to everlasting life, others to shame and everlasting contempt." Daniel 12:2 NIV

3) Orthodox Jews believe that the physical body will be resurrected, intact, in the messianic age. Because of this, the body shouldn't be cut after death (autopsies are frowned upon) and cremation is forbidden. A Jewish cemetery is called the 'House of Life' (Bet ha-Chaim), which reaffirms the view that the body will be resurrected.
4) Reform Jews believe that the body is simply a vessel for the soul, and reject the idea of physical resurrection. So Reform Jews accept cremation and organ donation.

Okay, it was wrong. But everlasting contempt seems a bit over the top.

Modern Judaism Teaches about Gan Eden and Gehinnom

1) Modern Jews believe in an afterlife spent in places called Gan Eden ("Garden of Eden" or Paradise) and Gehinnom (a bit like Purgatory), but they don't tend to have firm beliefs on the specifics of the afterlife.
2) Some see Gan Eden as a physical place of lavish banquets and warm sunshine. But others have a more spiritual view of it — as a closeness to God. Similarly, there are different views of Gehinnom — a place of fire and physical torment, or a chance to see missed opportunities and the harm a person caused in life.
3) Only if you've lived a blameless life will you be sent straight to Gan Eden when you die.
4) Most souls are sent to Gehinnom for a period of punishment and purification first, which many think lasts no longer than 12 months, before ascending to Gan Eden. Only the truly wicked never reach Paradise, but there are various ideas about what happens to them, e.g. they're annihilated, or they stay in Gehinnom forever.

The Shadows — they used to be Cliff Richard's band...

Yep, in the old days, when Cliff Richard was a young rock 'n' roll singer (well before he started doing all that Christmas nonsense), he had a backing band called the Shadows. But an eternity spent listening to Cliff Richard songs probably isn't what early Jews had in mind when they came up with Sheol...

Abortion and the Christian View

General & Christianity

Abortion is a subject that people often hold very strong views about.
And as you'd probably expect, religions have strong views about it too.

Abortion — Terminating a Pregnancy

1) Abortion is when a foetus is removed prematurely from the womb, before it is able to survive.
2) Abortion has been legal in England, Scotland and Wales since 1967. It can take place up till the 24th week of pregnancy, as long as two doctors agree that it's required. They must consider the quality of life of the woman, the unborn child, and any children the mother may already have.

There are complicated arguments for and against abortion...

i) The 'pro-choice' argument says that a woman has a right to choose what happens to her body (and since the foetus isn't independent of the woman, this argument says it must be considered part of the woman).
ii) But is it right to consider the foetus part of the mother when it's genetically different?
iii) Although many people are generally against abortion (seeing it as the taking of a life) they will agree that in certain circumstances, abortion should be permitted, e.g. if the mother's or child's health is at risk, if a woman has become pregnant through rape, or if a mother is too young to cope with a child.
iv) The question of when life actually begins is important here, too. Is it at conception (as the Roman Catholic Church says)? Or at birth? And is a foetus an actual person, or just a potential person?

The 'Sanctity of Life' Argument

Probably the most important biblical passage regarding the Sanctity of Life argument is the sixth of the Ten Commandments, "You shall not murder." — Exodus 20:13 NIV

1) Christianity, Islam and Judaism teach that all life is created by God. As God's creation, all life belongs to God and is therefore holy. This is the 'sanctity of life' argument.
2) Based on this, many religious people believe that we don't have the right to interfere with when life ends, or to prevent the beginning of a new life.

Many Christians see Abortion as Undesirable

1) Abortion is a very complicated and emotional issue, but generally speaking, Christianity teaches that abortion is undesirable. However, the Roman Catholic Church goes so far as to say that abortion is murder.
2) Not all Christian churches see it in such 'black-and-white' terms, however. The Church of England believes that abortion is permissible in certain circumstances, while the Religious Society of Friends (the Quakers) argues that the life of the unborn child cannot be valued above that of the woman.
3) Indeed, many Christians argue that allowing a woman to choose is a way of showing Christian compassion — whether they agree with the choice made or not.
4) Although the Bible doesn't actually mention abortion, other Christian writings (e.g. the Didache, a 2nd century manual of Christian teaching) are quite specifically against it.

"Abortion has been considered to be murder since the first centuries of the Church, and nothing permits it to be considered otherwise." — Pope Paul VI (Leader of Roman Catholic Church, 1970)

Church of the Blessed Virgin Mary

It's tricky, emotional stuff...

There are no easy answers. So learn the stuff on the page, and be ready to give both sides of the argument.

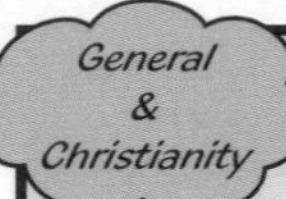

Euthanasia and the Christian View

Another complicated subject...

Euthanasia is often called Mercy Killing

Euthanasia means killing someone painlessly to relieve suffering, especially from an incurable illness. It's often called mercy killing.

1) There are two forms of euthanasia — voluntary euthanasia and non-voluntary euthanasia.
2) Voluntary euthanasia is when an ill person actively requests assistance to die, or refuses treatment which is keeping them alive, i.e. the person decides that they want to die and seeks help to achieve this.
3) Non-voluntary euthanasia is when the patient is unable to make such a request, and the decision is made by someone else — usually doctors and family members.
4) Suicide is when someone takes their own life — usually because of depression or illness. Attempted suicide used to be a crime in the UK, but it's now seen as a sign that someone needs help.
5) Assisted suicide is when a doctor provides someone with the means to end their own life, usually by prescribing a lethal dose of medication.

Euthanasia is Illegal in the UK

1) Euthanasia and assisted suicide are illegal in the UK, but euthanasia is allowed in certain circumstances in Albania, Belgium, Luxembourg, and the Netherlands, and assisted suicide is legal in Switzerland.
2) The charity 'Dignity in Dying' believes that many people would be grateful for 'the mercy of a painless death', and many people want assisted suicide legalised in the UK. In the 2005 British Social Attitudes Survey, 80% of people said they were in favour of letting terminally ill patients die with a doctor's help.
3) Legalisation would mean that scarce medical resources could be saved for people who could be cured.
4) A few doctors have even admitted helping patients to die, sometimes by giving a patient an excess of painkillers, which can ease suffering but can also lead to eventual death — this is known as 'double effect', which is legal so long as the intention was to relieve pain.
5) However, there is a concern that if euthanasia were legalised, the elderly may feel under pressure to end their life, even if they don't want to.

"Your Body is a Temple of the Holy Spirit"

1) The passage in the subheading (from 1 Corinthians NIV) suggests that God lives within each of us. Life is seen as a sacred gift, and so both euthanasia and suicide are seen as wrong by many Christians (see page 13 — the 'Sanctity of Life' argument).
2) Roman Catholics are the most strongly opposed to euthanasia. They believe that anything which intentionally causes death is 'a grave violation of the law of God'.

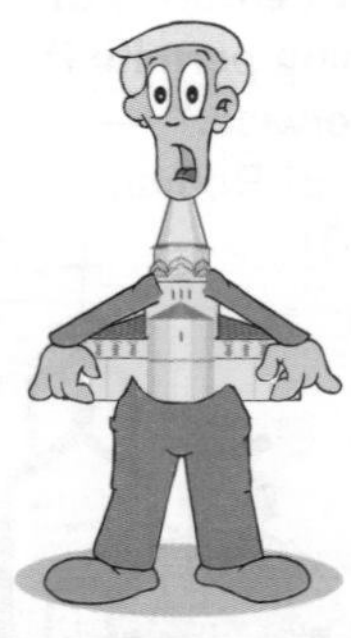

3) However, many Christians suggest that the easing of suffering is a way of demonstrating Christian compassion, and that the use of 'extraordinary treatment' (e.g. life-support machines) to keep a person alive is not always the best approach.
4) Most Anglican denominations agree that terrible distress should not be suffered at all costs, and that death may be considered a blessing. They argue that the quality of life (how worthwhile and enjoyable it is to live) must also be considered.
5) Local churches often have links with hospices. A hospice is a place where terminally ill people can be cared for, and can discuss any fears they may have about death.

I told you it was complicated...

It's also worth knowing about active and passive euthanasia. Passive euthanasia is stopping doing something that's keeping a person alive, e.g. turning off a life-support machine. Active euthanasia is actively causing the person to die, e.g. by giving a lethal injection. Some people accept passive, but not active, euthanasia.

Abortion & Euthanasia

Islam & Judaism

Muslims and Jews also have mixed opinions on these issues...

Abortion and Euthanasia — The Islamic View

Muslims believe that Allah created the world and everything in it. Our lives are sacred (see the 'Sanctity of Life' argument on p13). This means that abortion and euthanasia are generally seen as wrong.

Slay not your Children...

"And do not kill your children for fear of poverty. We provide for them and for you. Indeed, their killing is ever a great sin." — Qur'an 17:31

1) The passage on the right sums up Islamic teaching on abortion. Although there are circumstances in which it is permissible.
2) When the mother's life is in danger, abortion is seen as lawful. The potential life in the womb is not as important as the actual life of the mother.
3) Within the first 120 days, abortion can also be allowed if the baby would be born with a serious defect (though not all Muslims agree with this). After 120 days, abortion is only allowed to save the life of the mother.
4) Some Muslim women argue that they should be free to choose what happens to their bodies. Those that disagree claim that in the Qur'an it says that unborn children will want to know why they were killed.

Allah knows Why we Suffer...

Allah even has a plan for you, Norman Shuffleploppy.

1) Euthanasia is seen as wrong by most Muslims — because our lives are Allah's.
2) Muslims believe that Allah has a plan for every living person — he has decided how long each of us will live on this Earth and we do not have the right to interfere with that plan.
3) Islam teaches that life on Earth is a test. Allah knows why we suffer, and we do not have good reason to end our own lives, no matter how bad that suffering is.
4) Instead, those who are suffering should turn to Allah, pray and 'patiently persevere' — Allah is merciful, and all will be revealed on the Day of Judgement.

Abortion and Euthanasia — The Jewish View

"Be fruitful and increase in number... fill the earth." Genesis 1:28 NIV

"There is no god besides me. I put to death and I bring to life" Deuteronomy 32:39 NIV

1) As a general rule, Judaism is opposed to abortion, contraception and euthanasia — the passages on the right are often used to support this view.
2) However, Judaism does not believe that the life of an unborn child is more valuable than that of the mother. Many Jews accept that, in certain cases, abortion should be allowed. Most rabbis allow abortion if pregnancy becomes physically or mentally dangerous for the woman concerned, or if the child is likely to be severely disabled and unable to lead a full life. But it cannot simply be carried out for convenience.
3) Reform rabbis are more likely to allow abortion than Orthodox ones.

Only God can Decide when we Die

1) Jewish teaching is, generally, opposed to the practice of euthanasia — life is seen as a gift from God and is therefore sacred. We do not have the right to decide when a life should end.
2) However, the relief of pain and suffering is a key part of Jewish teaching. So although euthanasia is seen as wrong if it involves actively doing something to cause someone's death, it may be possible to withhold treatment, if this treatment was causing further distress.
3) The words of Rabbi Moses Isserles are sometimes used to argue that it may be reasonable to switch off a life-support machine that's keeping someone alive.

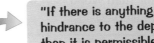

"If there is anything which causes a hindrance to the departure of the soul... then it is permissible to remove it."

Good lord — it's not like maths, is it...

I mean, in maths, things are true or false, right or wrong, black or white... with this it's all shades of grey.

General & Christianity

World Poverty: Christianity

Poverty causes great suffering in the world. So its causes and effects are of great concern for Christians.

Poverty Occurs for a Number of Reasons

1) The Brandt Report in 1980 identified an imbalance between the developed and the developing worlds. The developed world contains around 25% of the world's population but around 80% of the wealth. Little has changed since 1980.
2) Causes of poverty in the Third World include population growth, war, and the sale of raw materials at low prices. In the UK causes of poverty range from unemployment and homelessness to gambling.
3) Although possessing wealth is not against Christian teaching, occupations which may bring suffering to others are disapproved of — e.g. working in the arms trade, sex industry, or gambling industry.

Christians have a Duty to Relieve Poverty

"Rich nations have a grave moral responsibility towards those which are unable to ensure the means of their development by themselves..." from the Catechism of the Catholic Church: paragraph 2439

1) All Christian denominations have become more concerned with a fairer distribution of wealth. A key question is whether wealth ultimately belongs to God, and should therefore be for the good of everyone.
2) Charity is an important part of Christianity, and a concern for Christians is whether or not they should be wealthy. Though Jesus spoke of giving up wealth to help the poor, being wealthy is not against Christian teaching. Indeed, the Roman Catholic and Orthodox Churches (and to a lesser extent the Church of England) are extremely rich institutions — this is a worry for some believers.

"...the love of money is a root of all kinds of evil." 1 Timothy 6:10 NIV

3) A number of Christian organisations exist to tackle poverty — both in the UK and on a global level. These include Christian Aid and CAFOD:

CASE STUDY — CHRISTIAN AID

Christian Aid was set up after World War II to help refugees. It now has over 40 member organisations in the UK and Ireland, and works globally to relieve poverty. It raises money through donations, events and collections.

Most of Christian Aid's work is in development. Although they do contribute to emergency disaster relief, they believe the best way to help people is by 'helping them to help themselves'. They set up projects in the developing world, drawing on the skills of local people.

Development projects set up by Christian Aid aim to help with problems such as poor sanitation, education and healthcare, as well as encouraging the use of birth control. The organisation also aims to change government policy to help reduce the suffering of the world's poor, e.g. through debt relief, and fair-trade products.

CASE STUDY — CAFOD (CATHOLIC AGENCY FOR OVERSEAS DEVELOPMENT)

CAFOD was set up by the Catholic Bishops of England and Wales in 1962 to draw together a lot of small-scale development projects that were going on at the time.

They raise money through 'fast days' and other fund-raising activities.

Their guiding principle is that 'all human beings have a right to dignity and respect, and that the world's resources are a gift to be shared equally by all men and women, whatever their race, nationality or religion'.

CAFOD campaigns for Third World debt relief, effective financial aid for developing countries and fairer international trade rules.

Well I think exams are the root of all evil...

You need to know about a Christian organisation working to relieve world poverty — Christian Aid and CAFOD are just two examples. You choose one you're interested in.

World Poverty: Islam and Judaism

Islam and Judaism have similar views on poverty. Both believe it's our duty to look after those less fortunate than ourselves, and both expect people to give some of their income to the poor and needy.

Judaism says, "...do not be hardhearted or tightfisted..."

1) The above passage from Deuteronomy (NIV) sums up Jewish teaching on poverty. Maimonides said that the best way to give was "to help a person help themselves so that they may become self-supporting".
2) There are two main ways of giving to charity — Tzedakah and Gemilut Hasadim:

TZEDAKAH: Tzedakah is financial aid — even the poorest in society are expected to contribute 10% of their wealth. All wealth belongs to God, and not giving to the poor deprives them of what they're owed.

GEMILUT HASADIM: This refers to kind and compassionate actions towards those in need.

3) Many Jewish homes have collection boxes (called pushkes) in which money for charity can be placed. Children are encouraged to use these boxes — maybe donating some of their pocket money each week.
4) Although Judaism doesn't teach that everyone should try to be wealthy, it does suggest that extreme poverty will make others responsible for you, and that the love of wealth may turn you from God.

5) Unfairness and dishonesty in business are condemned — you're answerable to God for any wrongdoing.

CASE STUDY — TZEDEK (JEWISH ACTION FOR A JUST WORLD)

Tzedek is a Jewish charity set up in the UK that works with poor people of all races and religions, 'providing direct support to small scale sustainable self-help development projects for the relief and elimination of poverty'.

Their focus is on helping local projects, e.g. health and agriculture training schemes, that improve a community's ability to get itself out of poverty and achieve a better standard of living.

The Islamic View is Very Similar

1) In Islam, the principle is much the same — greed and waste are frowned upon and possessions ultimately belong to Allah.
2) Muslims are encouraged to act responsibly and help those in need.
3) Gambling is forbidden, and moneylending is seen as immoral if those in debt are being exploited through the charging of interest. Some Islamic banks exist to get around this.
4) Again, there are two main ways to help the disadvantaged — Zakah and Sadaqah:

ZAKAH: This is one of the Five Pillars of Islam — 2.5% of your yearly savings should be given to the needy, no matter how rich or poor you are.

SADAQAH: This is additional aid — maybe financial donations, or an act of compassion and love.

CASE STUDY — MUSLIM AID

Muslim Aid provides disaster relief and development aid around the world.

They aim to provide not only initial emergency aid after a war or natural disaster, but ongoing help to get people back on their feet. This help includes building new permanent housing, sanitation and schools, and offering small interest-free loans to help start-up businesses.

It all sounds like good advice to me...

Both Islam and Judaism teach that we have a responsibility to the planet, its resources and our fellow man. We are stewards of the Earth and should not exploit what we have been given at the expense of others.

Christianity, Islam & Judaism

The Media: Life and Death

There are a lot of sensitive issues in this section, and many people feel very strongly about them.

The Media Sometimes Criticise Religious Views

1) Life and death issues are important to everyone, so they tend to crop up a lot in the media — from in-depth documentaries to soap operas.
2) But the media is often accused of insensitivity to religious views — so the big question is this: "Should the media be free to criticise what religions say about matters of life and death?"

Arguments For

- Freedom of speech. This is the most fundamental one. In the UK, we have the right to freedom of opinion and expression — as long as anything said about a person is true.
- Education. By covering all views of topics like euthanasia and abortion, the media can help educate people about their options, and the implications of their choices.
- Constructive questioning can help deepen a person's faith.

Arguments Against

- Insensitive coverage of these issues can be seen as causing unnecessary offence.
- Unbalanced coverage. E.g. the media is sometimes accused of having a pro-choice bias when it comes to abortion coverage.
- Exaggerated or untrue representations of beliefs can damage a person's faith or give religion a 'bad name'.

Example: "Million Dollar Baby"

1) Another question you might get asked in the exam is whether or not the presentation of a life and death issue in the media was fair to religious people and beliefs.
2) A good example is the 2004 film "Million Dollar Baby", which tackles the issue of euthanasia.

What it's about: A boxing coach (a Catholic) takes on a female boxer ("Million Dollar Baby") and guides her up through the ranks. An illegal move by an opponent leaves her paralysed from the neck down with no hope of recovery. She asks her coach to help her to die, which he does in the end. (Oh yes — it's a cheery film...)

The issue: Does the coach show love by helping his student to die at her request and with dignity, or is it murder and a mortal sin?

How the film tackles it:

1) The coach spends a long time talking to his confessor and wrestling with his conscience.
2) In the end, by helping "Boxing Baby" to die, the trainer goes against his religion.
3) The film deals with beliefs, relationships and people very sensitively.
4) It gives no clear-cut answers — the viewer is left to decide whether the coach should be condemned by God.

How the film was received: The film was critically acclaimed and won four Academy Awards. But anti-euthanasia campaigners, including the bioethicist Wesley J. Smith, criticised the film for encouraging the euthanasia of disabled people.

There's nothing like a nice cheery end to a section...

You can choose any example from TV, radio, film or the national press for the exam. Whichever example you pick, you need to be able to answer these questions: What 'life and death' issues does it tackle? Was it fair to religious people? Did it cause offence to religious people and why?

Practice Questions

You're right... there's some heavy stuff in this section. And some of it's very topical — many of the issues in this section make it on to the telly pretty frequently in one way or another. For sure, when it comes to the exam, all this extra knowledge from the newspapers and the TV is useful. But there's no getting away from the fact that you also need to be able to present the religious viewpoints — even if it's only to say why you disagree with them.

So try your hand at these questions. And keep trying them until you can do them all without breaking into even the mildest of sweats.

1) What is:
   a) a near-death experience?
   b) the paranormal?
   c) resurrection?
   d) reincarnation?
   e) immortality of the soul?
   f) akhirah? (Islam)
   g) barzakh? (Islam)
   h) al'Jannah? (Islam)
   i) abortion?
   j) euthanasia?
   k) assisted suicide?

You only need to know what the Arabic words mean if you're studying Islam (fairly obvious — but I thought I'd best say). Remember, these are worth 2 marks each.

2) For each of the following questions, give two reasons for your point of view.
   a) Do you think there is a life after death?
   b) Do you agree with abortion?
   c) Do you agree with voluntary euthanasia?
   d) Do you think religious people should give up their wealth to help the poor?

These questions aren't asking for a balanced argument, just two good reasons for one opinion. Each reason's worth 2 marks in the exam.

3) For these questions, you need to express yourself as clearly as possible — make sure your writing is correct, accurate and well organised.
   a) Explain how non-religious experiences might lead to belief in a life after death.
   b) Choose one religion and explain how and why followers of the religion may differ in their beliefs about life after death.
   c) Choose one religion and explain how a belief in life after death affects the way its followers lead their lives.
   d) Explain why many Christians are against euthanasia.
   e) Explain how one religious agency is working to reduce world poverty.

These 8-mark questions can make a big difference to your grade. Have a look at p.39 for some advice on answering them.

4) Read the following statements:
   a) "Everyone's soul will be rewarded or punished in the afterlife."
   b) "Religious people shouldn't allow abortion."
   c) "Only God should be allowed to decide when we die."
   d) "Religious people have a responsibility to relieve world poverty."
   e) "Religious views on matters of life and death are sacred, and the media shouldn't be allowed to criticise them."

   For each statement:

   (i) Do you agree? Give reasons for your opinion.

   (ii) Give reasons why some people may disagree with you.

   In your answers you should refer to at least one religion.

It's 3 marks for one argument and 3 marks for the other. So for each part of the question you need three simple reasons, two detailed reasons or one really in-depth reason. And that means sitting down and learning the arguments properly.

Christianity, Islam, Judaism & General

Changing Attitudes to the Family

Marriage — a pretty big thing in anyone's life. Including yours if you get a question about it in the exam.

Marriage in the UK — Times are Changing

1) The number of marriages in the UK per year has been decreasing for at least thirty years.
2) At the same time, it's become more popular (and acceptable) for couples to cohabit (i.e. live together) — either instead of getting married, or as a 'trial marriage' before doing it for real. (However, government statistics seem to show that a marriage is more likely to break down if the couple lived together first.)
3) But there are also signs that things are changing, and that marriage is becoming more popular again.

Family Life in the UK is also Changing

1) There used to be two basic types of family that 'society' and the Christian Church considered 'ideal' — the nuclear family, and the extended family.
2) A nuclear family consists of parents and children. An extended family is where three or more generations live together or as close neighbours.

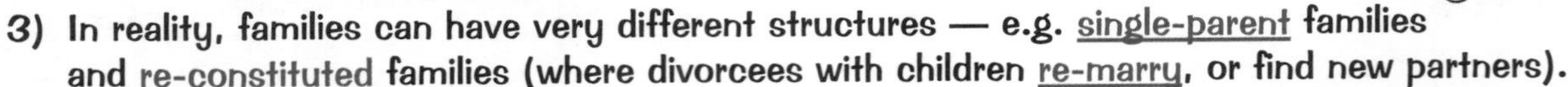

3) In reality, families can have very different structures — e.g. single-parent families and re-constituted families (where divorcees with children re-marry, or find new partners).

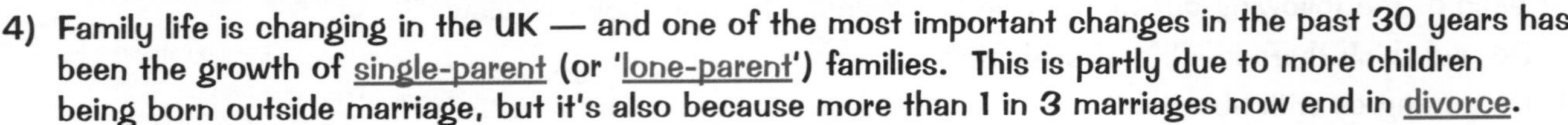

4) Family life is changing in the UK — and one of the most important changes in the past 30 years has been the growth of single-parent (or 'lone-parent') families. This is partly due to more children being born outside marriage, but it's also because more than 1 in 3 marriages now end in divorce.

Family is Important to Christians, Jews and Muslims

The Importance of the Family to Christians

1) Family life is seen as very important by most Christians — it's believed to be better for a child to have a father and a mother present (ideally the child's biological parents), so that he or she grows up with one role model of each sex.
2) Ideally, a stable family can give a child a sense of identity and a feeling of security, teaching him or her how to behave in different social situations, and how to give and receive love.
3) Many Christian churches offer help in raising children through Sunday schools. These schools aim to teach Christian morals and ideals by studying Bible stories.

The Importance of the Family to Muslims

1) Muslims believe that a stable family life teaches people to be kind, considerate and affectionate towards others, and that it's the duty of the father to raise his children as Muslims.
2) Local Mosques often have schools (Madrasahs) to help teach children the ways of Islam. There they learn Arabic so that they can read and understand the Qur'an, and are taught from the Hadith (the sayings of Muhammad) and Sunnah (the actions and way of life of Muhammad).

The Importance of the Family to Jews

1) Family life is also very important to Jews, as it's through the family that the Jewish religion and customs are passed on. Children take part in Shabbat rituals (the special meals and prayers of the day of rest) at home from an early age.
2) At a Jewish school called a Cheder, children learn Hebrew, and study the Torah and Talmud (a collection of teachings and commentaries).

Familililililililily — it's... erm... an extended family...*

So family life is changing, but it's still really important. And even though marriage might not be such a big deal these days, still about 50% of women and 40% of men in the UK marry before they're 30.

* Sorry, but it was either that or the "nuclear family" joke — take your pick.

Marriage and Divorce: Christianity

Christianity

Christians say Marriage Should be Forever

1) The Christian faith values marriage very highly — the joining of husband and wife in holy matrimony reflects the union of Jesus with his followers.
2) Jesus taught that marriage should be a lifelong union — marriage is seen as a covenant or contract between two people, involving commitment and responsibility. Christianity teaches that the purpose of marriage is for two people to offer love and mutual support and for procreation (to have children).
3) The Church recognises that not everyone is called to marriage (e.g. Roman Catholic priests) and from these people it demands celibacy.

"...a man will leave his father and mother and be united to his wife, and the two will become one flesh." Mark 10:7-8 NIV

"You shall not commit adultery." Exodus 20:14 NIV

In Ephesians 5:21-33, wives are encouraged to submit to their husbands, and husbands to love their wives, laying down their lives for them as Christ laid down his.

BIBLICAL TEACHING ON MARRIAGE

1) Marriage must be faithful. Neither person may have sex with anyone else — this would be adultery.
2) Marriage must be worked at — you have to keep on forgiving.
3) Marriage reflects Christ's love for his followers, and involves submission.

A Christian Wedding has Legal, Social and Religious Features

Most Christian weddings take place in church. The details will vary according to tradition and denomination, but all combine legal, social and religious features.

1. Hymns
2. Opening Statement explaining to the couple the seriousness of their vows
3. Declaration the couple and witnesses state there is no reason why they can't marry
4. Vows
5. Giving of ring(s) as a symbol of their lifelong commitment
6. Proclamation that the couple are now married
7. Prayers calling on God to bless the marriage
8. Signing of the register to make it legal
9. Closing worship

In an Orthodox wedding, crowns are placed on the heads of the bride and groom.

A Roman Catholic wedding may also include nuptial mass.

Christian Churches have Different Attitudes to Divorce

1) The breakdown of a marriage is seen by all Christians as a tragedy. However not all Christians agree about whether divorce is permissible, or even possible.

The Roman Catholic Church states that it is actually impossible to divorce. Marriage is a sacrament — God has made the couple into one flesh, and this cannot be undone. However, a marriage can be annulled — annulment means that it was never a true marriage in the first place. This can happen if:

i) either partner did not consent to the marriage or didn't understand what marriage is about,
ii) the couple didn't or couldn't have sex, or one partner refused to have children.

The Church of England states that divorce is possible and accepts that some marriages fail. Divorced people can only re-marry in church if they can find a minister willing to marry them, but this doesn't satisfy every member of the Church.

Nonconformist Churches (e.g. Baptists and Methodists) will generally re-marry divorcees, but an individual minister can refuse to do so if this goes against his or her own conscience.

2) Jesus himself was anti-divorce, but pro-forgiveness.

In Mark 10:2-12 Jesus says that Moses allowed divorce because of people's 'hardness of heart'. But he says that marriages were meant to last for life, and if a divorcee re-marries it's the same as committing adultery.

In John 8:1-11, Jesus freely forgives a woman caught in the act of adultery. But he tells her, 'Go now and leave your life of sin' (NIV).

Matthew 19:8-9 says that divorce and remarriage are only permitted to someone whose partner has been unfaithful.

3) But some Christians view an unhappy marriage as a waste of two lives, and so see divorce as preferable. It's also argued that parents fighting can harm the emotional wellbeing of children more than a divorce.

Don't let all this trouble and strife get you down...

Divorce is an issue that you might feel very strongly about — but make sure you learn the full range of views.

Islam

Marriage and Divorce: Islam

Marriage is very important in Islam. Muslims are advised to marry, and Muhammad himself was married.

Marriage is Recommended for Three Reasons

1) Marriage provides companionship.
2) Marriage provides a secure environment for having children (procreation) and bringing them up as practising Muslims.
3) The sexual instinct is very strong and needs to be carefully channelled.

See page 24 for more about marriage in Islam.

"...He created for you from yourselves mates that you may find tranquillity in them; and He placed between you affection and mercy..." — Qur'an 30:21

"Whoever among you can marry, should marry, because it helps him lower his gaze and guard his modesty." — Prophet Muhammad (Sahih Bukhari)

Choosing a Partner is often your Parents' Responsibility

Practising Muslims generally want their children to marry other Muslims. Islam affects a Muslim's whole life, and being married to a non-Muslim could create tension, especially with bringing up children.

1) Most Muslims believe it's unwise for young men and women to mix freely, and 'dating' is discouraged or even forbidden.
2) In most Muslim communities, parents search for suitable partners for their children — i.e. Muslims often have 'arranged marriages'.
3) However, as marriage is a contract, both partners must consent to it.
4) Parents also have a responsibility to help if the marriage begins to go wrong.

The Marriage Ceremony — Customs Vary

The marriage ceremony is different in different Islamic cultures, but there's always a religious ceremony (witnessed by Allah) and a public one (witnessed by the community). They usually go like this...

1) A nikah (contract) is drawn up in advance by the families of the bride and groom, and a mahr (dowry) paid by the groom to the bride.
2) An imam (leader of prayers) is often present (though this isn't compulsory).
3) Vows are exchanged, and a marriage declaration is made by each partner. A Hadith (prophetic saying) or a khutbah (speech) may also be said.
4) There will be a big feast afterwards, though the men and women may enjoy this separately.

Divorce is the Last Resort

"Of all the lawful acts the most detestable to Allah is divorce." — Prophet Muhammad (Sunan Abu Dawud)

1) Divorce is permitted, but only as a very last resort. If things aren't going well, an arbiter from each family should be appointed to try to sort things out.
2) Muslims see reconciliation as particularly important when the couple have children.
3) But, in Islam, marriage is a contract and like any other contract it can be ended.
4) When the man says 'I divorce you' three times, the marriage is said to be over. However, there's often a period of three months after the first of these declarations. This allows time for reflection, and also to ensure that the woman is not pregnant.

This kind of divorce isn't legal in the UK, as Islamic law isn't part of the British legal system.

5) A woman can divorce a man in this way (divorce 'by talaq') if it was written into her marriage contract. Otherwise she has to apply to a Shari'ah court for a divorce 'by khul'.
6) After divorce, both men and women are free to re-marry.

But I never said I wanted to study a foreign language...

There are quite a lot of Arabic words in these Islam sections — and they're in the syllabus too, so you need to know 'em. The same goes for the sections on Judaism — they contain quite a bit of Hebrew. So if your RS teacher never told you what you were letting yourself in for, it's too late to complain now.

Marriage and Divorce: Judaism

Judaism

Traditionally all Jews have been expected to marry and have at least two children — a boy and a girl.

Marriage Matters in Judaism

1) To Jews, marriage is an emotional, intellectual and spiritual union. It is seen as the proper context for sex (seen as natural and God-given) and having children (procreation), but is also for companionship.
2) It's the Jewish custom for parents to arrange for their children to meet suitable partners. To help in this it was common to use a 'shadchan', or matchmaker (and it still is among the ultra-Orthodox).
3) Although 40% of UK Jews 'marry out' (i.e. marry non-Jews), those who take their religion seriously find this worrying — children of 'mixed marriages' are less likely to be brought up as observant Jews. Some Jews see this as a threat to Judaism's survival, and even a 'posthumous victory to Hitler'.

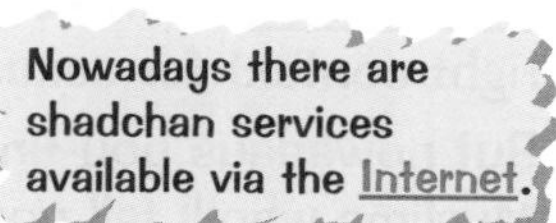

Nowadays there are shadchan services available via the Internet.

Kiddushin is the First Part of the Marriage Ceremony

'Kiddushin' is the first part of the marriage ceremony, and is usually translated as 'betrothal'. The word comes from a root meaning sanctified, which reflects the holiness of marriage.

Different Jewish communities celebrate marriage in different ways, but there are some common features.

1) The ceremony takes place beneath a chuppah, a wedding canopy — this is a piece of cloth supported by four poles. It is thought the cloth represents privacy, and the open sides hospitality.
2) Usually, the bride will circle the groom seven times.
3) The groom gives the bride a ring and makes the betrothal declaration: 'Behold you are consecrated to me with this ring according to the laws of Moses and Israel.' This completes the kiddushin.
4) Then the ketubah (marriage contract) is read out. The traditional ketubah sets out the woman's right to be cared for by her husband and her entitlement in the event of divorce (a bit like a modern prenuptial agreement). Reform Jews have rewritten the ketubah to be a mutual statement of love and commitment, more like Christian marriage vows.
5) The sheva brachot or seven blessings are said — normally by a rabbi, who usually conducts the service.
6) The groom breaks a glass with his foot in memory of the destruction of the Temple in Jerusalem by the Romans in 70 CE. It's said that there can never be complete joy for the Jewish people until the Temple is restored — this is why it's remembered.
7) After the service there will be a festive meal and dancing, and shouts of 'mazel tov!' (good luck, best wishes). Among some Orthodox Jews, the men and women dance separately.

Divorce is a Last Resort

1) Judaism accepts that some marriages don't work out, and that it's better for a couple to divorce than to stay together in bitterness. But divorce is a very last resort after all attempts at reconciliation have failed.
2) Traditionally, a woman cannot initiate divorce, but a divorce does require the wife's consent.
3) In Reform synagogues, if the husband will not grant his wife a certificate of divorce, a 'Get', the Bet Din (Jewish court) can do so, freeing her to re-marry.
4) In Orthodox synagogues, women who want a divorce but whose husbands will not grant one (or who aren't around to grant one) are known as 'agunot' — chained women.

Go on, learn it all — and I'll give you a Scooby-snack...

Rrrokay... Christian, Jewish and Muslim teachings about marriage and morality have a lot in common. This isn't so surprising — all three religions share the same Near Eastern background. And can I just say how nice it is to have a few happy pages after some of the previous ones in this book. (Apart from the divorce bits, that is.)

General

Religious Attitudes to Sex

Christianity, Islam and Judaism have all formulated laws concerned with sex. But this doesn't mean that religious people think there is anything wrong or dirty about having sex — quite the opposite.

Christianity, Islam and Judaism have a Lot in Common...

The three faiths have a lot in common when it comes to sex.

1) Traditionally all three religions have believed that the only right context for sexual activity is within marriage.
2) But nowadays you find liberal Christians, Jews and Muslims who'll tell you that this belief is outdated.
3) 'Orthodox' members of all faiths say that certain moral principles never change, however.

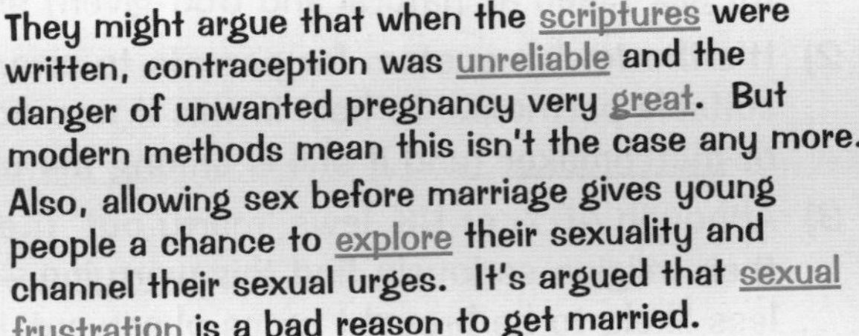
They might argue that when the scriptures were written, contraception was unreliable and the danger of unwanted pregnancy very great. But modern methods mean this isn't the case any more. Also, allowing sex before marriage gives young people a chance to explore their sexuality and channel their sexual urges. It's argued that sexual frustration is a bad reason to get married.

4) All three religions teach that couples should wait until they are married, rather then having pre-marital sex. In fact, it's very important to most Muslims that people, especially girls, remain virgins until marriage.
5) The Christian Church teaches that the total giving of self in sex shouldn't be treated casually — self-control and sexual restraint are considered important. Christians are urged to keep sex within marriage for positive reasons more than negative ones — marriage is believed to give sex a special status.
6) Promiscuity (having many sexual partners) is seen as wrong in all three religions — in Christianity it's seen as dishonouring yourself.

...but they're Not Identical

1) Judaism and Christianity are monogamous — adultery is forbidden by the Commandments.
2) Islam permits, but doesn't encourage, polygamy. A man may have up to four wives, but only if he can support them and treat them equally.

Muhammad actually had eleven wives during his lifetime — although not all at the same time.

Homosexuality — Scriptures say it's Wrong

Homosexuality means being attracted to members of the same sex.

1) Homosexuality is seen in other species, and many non-religious people see it as a natural alternative to heterosexuality.
2) But the scriptures of all three religions seem to say that homosexual sex is wrong — although the relevant passages are interpreted differently by some people.
3) Some (including some priests) argue that the scriptures were written against a very different cultural background from ours, so we can't apply their standards today.

"Because of this, God gave them over to shameful lusts. Even their women exchanged natural relations for unnatural ones. In the same way the men also abandoned natural relations with women and were inflamed with lust for one another. Men committed indecent acts with other men, and received in themselves the due penalty for their perversion." — Romans 1:26-27 NIV

4) Christianity and Judaism no longer condemn homosexuality, but it isn't seen as the ideal and many still view homosexual sex as a sin. So many religious gays opt for celibacy (they don't have sexual relationships).
5) Civil partnerships became legal in the UK in December 2005. They give homosexual couples the same rights as married couples concerning things like custody of children.
6) The Church of England doesn't allow same-sex partnerships to be blessed in a church. However, there have been some cases where vicars have gone against this rule and blessed the unions of homosexual couples anyway.

7) Reform Jews allow commitment ceremonies for homosexuals — these can take place in a synagogue.
8) Homosexuality is strictly forbidden by Islamic Shari'ah law, so in many Muslim countries it's still illegal. In some countries, e.g. Iran and Saudi Arabia, homosexual acts between men carry the death penalty.

Oranges are not the only fruit, but that's all you're allowed to eat, apparently...

Oooh, here we go again... courting controversy. Whatever you think about this stuff yourself, you still need to know what the religions teach. Then you can agree or disagree with them all you like — it's up to you...

Contraception

Christianity, Islam, Judaism & General

Hmmm... another tricky topic...

Contraception — Preventing a Pregnancy

1) Contraception (or birth control) is anything that aims to prevent a woman becoming pregnant (conceiving).
2) Contraception can be temporary (e.g. the contraceptive pill, condoms) or permanent (sterilisation).
3) The Roman Catholic Church believes that preventing conception is against 'natural law' and that the use of any artificial contraception is a grave sin. Indeed, it teaches that humans have an obligation to 'be fruitful and increase in number'. Many individual Roman Catholics disagree with this, especially because of recent concerns about AIDS. The Church does allow natural family planning though — by only having sex at the times during a woman's cycle when she's less fertile.

4) Other Christian Churches have different views on the matter. The Anglican, Methodist and Presbyterian Churches are in favour of contraception, suggesting that it lets parents plan their family in a responsible way.
5) Many Christians believe that contraception should be a question of individual conscience.

Islam Teaches that Life is a Sacred Gift from Allah

1) The Qur'an encourages procreation and Muslims believe that conception is the will of Allah. So although contraception isn't specifically mentioned in the Qur'an, it's often seen as unwelcome.

"...He gives to whom He wills female [children], and He gives to whom He wills males ...and He renders whom He wills barren..." — Qur'an 42:49-50

2) Most Muslims feel that it's the right of both husband and wife to try for children, so both partners must agree to any contraception.
3) Different Muslims have different views on contraception, e.g. in Iran, contraception for family planning is actively encouraged. But more conservative scholars and clerics have campaigned against contraception.

In most Muslim countries, contraception is permitted if:

i) there's a threat to the mother's health,
ii) it could help a woman who already has children,
iii) there is a greater than average chance of the child being born with disabilities,
iv) the family is too poor to raise a child.

4) Only 'reversible' methods are allowed, though — permanent sterilisation and vasectomies are frowned on.

Jews Generally see Contraception as Bad

1) Judaism traditionally teaches that a child is a gift from God, and contraception interferes with God's plans to bless couples with children.
2) Most Orthodox Jews only accept contraception if pregnancy could be physically or psychologically harmful to the mother or an existing child.
3) Reform Jews are happier with the idea of contraception for family planning — leaving the decision of whether or not to use it to individual conscience. (Having said that, not wanting to have children isn't a good enough reason to use contraception for many Jews.)
4) Sex should be as natural as possible, though, so hormonal contraceptives like the contraceptive pill are generally preferred to barrier methods like condoms. But their use may be encouraged by some as a means of preventing the spread of HIV and other STIs (sexually transmitted infections).

Nothing's ever simple is it...

People interpret their religion's teachings in different ways, so it's difficult to give a clear-cut overview of what a religion teaches. These are very 'human' topics, and people are very different. But all these different opinions about various issues makes for plenty to say in the exam.

Christianity, Islam & Judaism

The Media: Marriage and Family

It's another media page — 'is nothing sacred!', I hear you cry. Erm... apparently not... no.

Soaps Tackle some Difficult Issues

1) In recent years, soap operas like "EastEnders" and "Hollyoaks" have covered (amongst other things) homosexuality, rape, prostitution, celibacy, incest, marriage and infidelity (although rarely in the same episode).
2) Even though soaps are often seen as a form of escapism, they let us see how a variety of characters deal with issues and emotions that we could all face at some point in our lives.
3) However, characters are sometimes criticised for being one-dimensional stereotypes. They can easily cause offence to people.

Don't you gow blaymin' 'er — you's ve one what ran off with moi bravva woile oi was still in 'ospital 'avin' me leg amputated after you burned the 'ouse down...again...and it caved in on me woile you was daan ve pab, off your 'ead — even though you was pregnant wiv' moi best mayte's kid...

An Example from Film: "Four Weddings and a Funeral"

"Four Weddings" is a great example for marriage and the family. It covers lots of different issues.

What it's about: It's a romantic comedy, but it asks lots of important questions about love, relationships and commitment. The plot centres around Charles, a single thirty-something, and his on-off relationship with Carrie, an American woman he meets at the film's first wedding. (If you haven't seen it, this is the perfect excuse to — it's a great film.)

The issues: Promiscuity, marriage and divorce, homosexuality, committed cohabitation.

Promiscuity:

Both the central characters are "serial monogamists" — they've had a string of different sexual partners. At one point in the film, Carrie admits to having had 33 different sexual partners. Some Christians might see this as sexually irresponsible and emotionally empty. But the film doesn't encourage this behaviour — Charles is shocked.

"Flee from sexual immorality. All other sins a man commits are outside his body, but he who sins sexually sins against his own body. Do you not know that your body is a temple of the Holy Spirit..." — 1 Corinthians 6:18-19 NIV

Marriage and divorce:

During the film, Carrie marries 'the wrong man' (a rich politician), which very soon ends in divorce. And Charles nearly marries 'the wrong woman' in a Church wedding. His brother stops him, because he knows Charles doesn't love her. This illustrates the importance of marrying for love.

Homosexuality:

For most of the film, the happiest, most committed relationship we see is that between Charles's two gay friends Gareth and Matthew. Their relationship is shown as a 'marriage', which ends suddenly when Gareth dies of a heart attack. The film challenges the idea that homosexual relationships are less committed or loving than heterosexual ones.

Committed cohabitation:

At the end of the film, Charles and Carrie decide to stay together and have children, but not get married. Religious liberals accept cohabitation in a stable and loving relationship, but hope that it will be a 'prelude' to marriage. Roman Catholics and many other religious conservatives believe that when you decide to commit to someone it should be inside marriage and open to having and raising children.

EastEnders — real life stuff or total pap? Cast your votes...

This is another of those "pick an issue that's been presented in one form of the media" jobbies, so if you don't watch soaps or you haven't seen "Four Weddings and a Funeral", pick something else. You have to be able to say which marriage and family issues it covers, and whether it tackled them in a fair way.

Practice Questions

Ding dong, ding dong, ding dong, ding dong... ah, don't you just love weddings. But as with most Religion and Life topics, it's not all champagne and roses. All three religions teach that marriage involves commitment and faithfulness, and that it's something that has to be worked at...
Speaking of which, hadn't you better get to work on these questions? Go on, off you go...

1) What is:
   a) a nuclear family?
   b) a re-constituted family?
   c) cohabitation?
   d) procreation?
   e) adultery?
   f) mahr? (Islam)
   g) the ketubah? (Judaism)
   h) kiddushin? (Judaism)
   i) promiscuity?
   j) a civil partnership?

Every question in the exam starts with defining a key term. If you don't learn the definitions (and they're all in the glossary), you're throwing away an easy 2 marks.

2) For each of the following questions, give two reasons for your point of view.
   a) Do you think marriage is important?
   b) Do you think divorcees should be allowed to re-marry in a Christian church?
   c) Do you think people should have sex before marriage?
   d) Do you agree with contraception?

These are pretty big questions, but remember they're only worth 4 marks in the exam. Just state an opinion and give two good reasons for holding it. You don't have to write an essay.

3) For these questions, you need to express yourself as clearly as possible — make sure your writing is correct, accurate and well organised.
   a) Explain how the structure of families in the UK has changed over the last 30 years.
   b) Explain why most Christians value marriage highly.
   c) Choose one religion and explain how its marriage ceremony reflects its religious teachings.
   d) Choose one religion and explain its teachings on divorce.
   e) Choose one religion and explain why some of the followers of that religion may be against the use of contraception.

If you're studying Christianity and a second religion, see if you can answer these questions for both religions — it's good practice. Remember, they're worth 8 marks in the exam.

4) Read the following statements:
   a) "Religion can help keep a family together."
   b) "Getting a divorce is better than living in an unhappy marriage."
   c) "Religious couples should keep sex within marriage."
   d) "Homosexuality is wrong."

   For each statement:

   (i) Do you agree? Give reasons for your opinion.

   (ii) Give reasons why some people may disagree with you.

   In your answers you should refer to at least one religion.

The easiest way to tackle these is to give a secular (non-religious) argument for one part of the question, and a religious counter argument. It doesn't matter which way round you put them, but your arguments have to be detailed enough to get you 3 marks each.

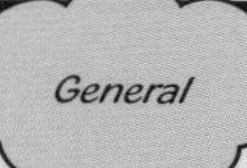

Prejudice and Equality

The world we live in is full of people from different religious, racial and cultural backgrounds. And the way each religion deals with this is important, as it can help or hinder the building of communities.

Prejudice has Many Causes

It's worth being very clear about what a few words mean...

Justice	the principle of fairness — both legally and more generally.
Equality	being equal, and being treated equally.
Community	the people living in a certain place, or a group of people with the same religious or cultural characteristics.
Prejudice	judging something or someone with no good reason, or without full knowledge of a situation.
Discrimination	unjust treatment, often resulting from prejudice.

1) Prejudice has many causes, and is often the product of early influences. It tends to be the result of widely held (yet inaccurate) beliefs of a particular community or family.
2) Discrimination comes in many forms... Individuals may discriminate by being violent and abusive. Whole societies may discriminate by passing laws which prevent certain people from doing certain things.

Racism is One Form of Prejudice

It's a sad fact that some people are prejudiced against anyone from a different cultural or religious background, or simply because of the colour of their skin.

1) There have been many instances of racial discrimination in the UK in recent years — usually as a result of ignorance, misunderstanding or segregation. At times these have culminated in rioting or murder.
2) Racism is often based on stereotypes — fixed and standardised images of groups of people, which can be used to promote negative thoughts and actions.
3) The media has an important role to play. Television and newspapers can educate — or help fuel negative stereotypes (see page 36).
4) More than 80% of all hate crime (crime driven by prejudice) is racially motivated. These racist crimes lead to further segregation and increased hostility within communities.

Racial segregation is when people of different races do their daily activities separately — either because they're forced to, or because it's the social norm.

The Government Tries to Promote Community Cohesion

1) The UK is a multi-ethnic, multi-faith society (see page 34), so it can be hard for members of a community to feel they have much in common — they can lack 'community cohesion'.
2) This is particularly true of places where there are lots of people from ethnic minorities.
3) The Government is trying to promote the idea of 'Britishness' as something that goes beyond racial and cultural differences to help tie communities together.
4) The Race Relations Act (1976) is part of this. It makes it illegal to discriminate on the grounds of race, colour or nationality, or to publish anything likely to cause racial hatred.

Sex Discrimination — it's also Illegal

Most societies have historically been male dominated, and have only started to change relatively recently.

1) Up until the middle of the 20th century, it was seen as a woman's role to marry, take care of the family home and raise children, while the men went out to work. The man was the head of the household, and his wife was expected to be obedient. After World War II, these attitudes started to change.
2) In 1975 the Sex Discrimination Act was passed by Parliament. This made it illegal to discriminate against people on account of their gender (sexism) — especially in the employment and education fields.

Community cohesion — you could always try superglue...

This is difficult and emotive stuff, but like all Religion and Life topics, it's not supposed to be easy...

Attitudes To Equality: Christianity

Christianity

For Christians, the Bible has plenty to say on the subject of equality...

The Bible has Plenty of 'Anti-Prejudice' Stories

1) The idea of 'do unto others as you would have them do unto you' is a fundamental part of Christian teaching (sometimes called the 'Golden Rule').
2) Generally Christians believe that everyone was created equal by God, and so they try to avoid discrimination and promote equality. They look to the example of Jesus, who told stories about equality, and acted true to his own teaching by mixing with a variety of people himself.
3) One of the most famous stories in the New Testament is the Parable of the Good Samaritan (Luke 10:25-37) where one man comes to the aid of another simply because he is suffering.
4) But there are plenty of other biblical verses preaching equal treatment for all — these two are from the New Testament.

The Parable of the Good Samaritan

A man is beaten up and left half-dead by robbers. First a priest and then a Levite (the Levites were a Jewish priestly tribe) walking down the road see him, but carry on walking. But a Samaritan (considered an enemy by the Jews) bandages the man, puts him on his donkey, takes him to an inn and sees that he is looked after.

"...there is no Greek or Jew... barbarian, Scythian, slave or free, but Christ is all, and is in all." Colossians 3:11 NIV

"My brothers... don't show favouritism. Suppose a man comes into your meeting wearing a gold ring and fine clothes, and a poor man in shabby clothes also comes in. If you show special attention to the man wearing fine clothes... but say to the poor man... 'Sit on the floor by my feet,' have you not... become judges with evil thoughts?" James 2:1-4 NIV

5) And Deuteronomy (a Book of Law in the Old Testament) includes these...

"Do not take advantage of a hired man who is poor and needy..." Deuteronomy 24:14 NIV

"Do not deprive the alien or the fatherless of justice..." Deuteronomy 24:17 NIV

By the way, 'alien' means 'foreigner' here.

Many People have Fought against Prejudice

1) Most Christians would argue that we should avoid prejudice on the basis of race, gender, religion, age, disability, colour or class. The Bible has plenty of specific teaching on these matters.

"...loose the chains of injustice and untie the cords of the yoke, to set the oppressed free... Then your light will break forth like the dawn..." Isaiah 58:6-8 NIV

2) There are many examples of individual Christians struggling against injustice — e.g.:

DIETRICH BONHOEFFER was a German Christian who felt the church had a duty to speak out against the Nazis' treatment of the Jews. He later became involved in an active conspiracy against the Nazi Party and was hanged in a concentration camp.

ARCHBISHOP DESMOND TUTU and BISHOP TREVOR HUDDLESTON were active in the fight against apartheid in South Africa (see next page).

DR MARTIN LUTHER KING was a Baptist minister who dedicated his life to trying to change the way black people were treated in the USA. He organised peaceful marches, rallies and boycotts, and in 1965 blacks were given equal voting rights with whites. King was assassinated in 1968 aged only 39.

The Good Samaritan — what a nice bloke...

This is a serious issue that often makes it into the news. And it's one that you might have personal experience of — and if you do, you can use that experience to help answer your exam question. But be careful not to just rant on about yourself — you'll need to refer to the religious teachings as well.

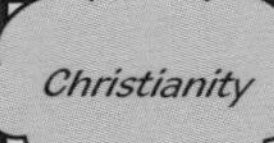

Attitudes To Equality: Christianity

Most Christian Churches Work to Promote Racial Harmony

1) Leviticus 19:33-34 contains some basic teaching on the way people from different races and cultural backgrounds should be treated.

"When an alien lives with you in your land, do not mistreat him... Love him as yourself..." Leviticus 19:33-34 NIV

This story's actually about foreigners living in Israel, but Christians argue that it also applies to the modern world.

2) There's a story about Simon Peter in Acts that's also relevant.

Acts 10:1-35 tells a story about Simon Peter. He is told by God not to consider impure anything that God has made. So when Cornelius, a Roman soldier, sends for Peter, Peter goes willingly, even though it is against the law for Jews to associate with non-Jews. Peter says, "...God does not show favouritism but accepts men from every nation..." (NIV)

3) The parable of the Good Samaritan (see previous page) is an example of Christian teaching on the treatment of people from other cultures. The Samaritans were a mixed race who suffered a great deal of discrimination at the time Jesus told the story.

4) More recently, Dr George Carey (the former Archbishop of Canterbury) spoke about the fundamental Christian belief that racism is wrong, that everyone is created in God's image.

"Racism has no part in the Christian Gospel... it contradicts our Lord's command... It solves no problems and creates nothing but hatred and fear." Dr George Carey

Not really what we were after, guys...

5) But although Christians generally work to improve racial harmony (people of all races living and working together peacefully), there have been occasions when this hasn't been the case...

The Dutch Reformed Church of South Africa (DRC) believed that God had divided mankind into different races and made white people superior. This idea became law in the system of apartheid.

Trevor Huddleston (an English bishop working in South Africa) argued that apartheid was against God's will. For nearly 50 years, he struggled against it using non-violent methods, until apartheid eventually ended in 1992.

Sex Discrimination — Not So Clear

1) The Bible gives different messages on the subject of sex discrimination. In the New Testament, women are found among Jesus' followers and he treated them equally — remarkable for the time.
2) But this is taken from St Paul's letter to his assistant Timothy:
3) Although in Galatians 3:28 St Paul writes, "There is neither... male nor female, for you are all one in Christ Jesus." (NIV)

"I do not permit a woman to teach or to have authority over a man; she must be silent. For Adam was formed first, then Eve... it was the woman who was deceived and became a sinner. But women will be saved through childbearing..."
1 Timothy 2:12-15 NIV

Women in the Christian Church

There's evidence from the Bible that women, as well as men, taught and led congregations in the very early Christian Church, e.g. Phoebe (Romans 16:1-2), Priscilla (Acts 18:26, 1 Corinthians 16:19, Romans 16:3), Mary, Tryphena and Tryphosa (Romans 16:12).

But for much of the Church's history, women haven't been allowed to be ordained as priests. The reasoning being that Jesus only called men to be Apostles.

Over the last 50 years, this has started to change — women can now be ordained as ministers in most Protestant denominations and as Anglican priests, but not as Roman Catholic or Orthodox priests.

Racism — still a big issue today, unfortunately...

In the UK prejudice against Muslims has increased in recent years. This has led to further mistrust and calls for segregation from some, and an increased desire for tolerance and integration from others.

Attitudes To Equality: Islam

Islam

Islam is truly international — with followers from many countries, and many ethnic and cultural backgrounds.

Islam says People are Created Equal, but not Identical

1) Islam teaches that all people were created by Allah, and were created equal (although not the same). He intended humanity to be created with differences. But this just means we're all individuals. Hurrah.

"And of His signs is the creation of the heavens and the earth and the diversity of your languages and your colours..." Qur'an 30:22

2) Muslims all over the world are united through the ummah — the community of Islam. The ummah consists of all Muslims, regardless of colour, nationality, tradition (i.e. Sunni or Shi'ite) and so on. This can help promote racial and social harmony, as no one is excluded or discriminated against in theory.

Most Muslims in the UK are from ethnic minorities, and so they're more likely to be subjected to racially motivated attacks, abuse and murder than their white neighbours. As a result, a number of peaceful pressure groups have been established — some working within Muslim communities, others working with the Government or with other faith groups.

3) Hajj (pilgrimage to Makkah) especially demonstrates equality. Those on pilgrimage all wear simple white garments, showing everyone's equal before Allah — wealth, status and colour don't matter.

4) The fact that all Muslims should pray five times a day at set times, and face Makkah whilst doing so, also demonstrates unity and equality. Men and women often pray together at home — however, they must pray in separate groups in the mosque.

The Qur'an teaches that Men and Women are Equal

1) Men and women have an equal obligation to Allah in terms of prayer, fasting, pilgrimage and charity. And all Muslims, male and female, are obliged to seek education:

"Indeed, the Muslim men and Muslim women, the believing men and believing women, the obedient men and obedient women... the charitable men and charitable women, the fasting men and fasting women... and the men who remember Allah often and the women who do so — for them Allah has prepared forgiveness and a great reward." Qur'an 33:35

2) In the early days of Islam, there were many female religious scholars.

3) But there are also some teachings that might be interpreted as meaning men are superior, e.g.

"Men are in charge of women by [right of] what Allah has given one over the other and what they spend [for maintenance] from their wealth..." Qur'an 4:34

Although they're usually taken to mean that men and women just have different roles within the community or family — men are responsible for providing for the family, and women are responsible for the home.

WOMEN AND THE MOSQUE

Women aren't encouraged to attend the mosque for prayer, but the Prophet Muhammad did permit it. If they do go to the mosque, they must pray in a separate group — behind (or otherwise out of sight of) the men.

Women are not permitted to lead the prayers of men, but they may lead other women. This is agreed by all traditional schools of Islam, both Sunni and Shi'ah.

Muslim feminist Asra Nomani is leading a campaign to end segregation in the mosque, and allow woman-led mixed-gender prayers. In 2005, Amina Wadud led a mixed-gender prayer in New York. Their actions have been condemned by Muslim scholars as not following the teachings of Islam.

Equal but not the same — don't try that one in maths...

In Islam, a woman's traditional role has been to create a halal homelife for the family, while the man went out to work and made sure the children were good Muslims. However, not all Muslims live in this traditional way. In some cultures there is almost complete equality between men and women.

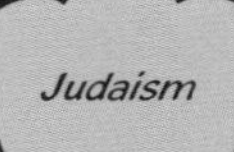

Attitudes To Equality: Judaism

Like Christianity and Islam, Judaism teaches that God created people equal.

The Hebrew Bible Preaches Tolerance

Racism is disapproved of in Judaism. The Hebrew Bible (the Old Testament) has a lot to say on the matter.

1) The Book of Genesis suggests that all of humanity comes from the same source and is, therefore, equal before God.

"Adam named his wife Eve, because she would become the mother of all the living." Genesis 3:20 NIV

2) Other messages of tolerance can be found in Deuteronomy 23:7, and Leviticus 19:33-34 (see p. 30).

"Do not abhor an Edomite, for he is your brother. Do not abhor an Egyptian, because you lived as an alien in his country." Deuteronomy 23:7 NIV

3) Deuteronomy 23 contains a discussion of who should be called 'the Lord's people'. This could be taken as meaning we should show tolerance for other nationalities. However, the same chapter does contain references to certain people or nations who should be excluded.
4) The Jewish people are sometimes called the 'chosen people'. This doesn't mean they think they're better than anyone else — simply that God gave them additional responsibilities.
5) The stories of Ruth and Jonah (both in the Hebrew Bible, i.e. the Old Testament) could also be used to promote social and racial harmony.

The Story of Jonah...

Jonah was told to preach to the people of Nineveh, who had upset God. When he preached God's message, the people of Nineveh were humble and repentant, which pleased God, and so God spared the city, upsetting Jonah. But God said he was right to spare the city, and that Jonah was wrong to be upset. The message is, If God can love and forgive, we should be able to live with others too.

First I get thrown off the boat, then I get eaten by a big fish. This must be a Monday.

Before he got to Nineveh, Jonah was swallowed by a big fish and stayed there for 3 days.

And Isaiah 42:6 shows that God does not want the Jews to turn their backs on non-Jews, but to be "a light for the Gentiles".

The Story of Ruth...

Naomi and her husband leave Judah because of a famine — they end up in Moab. Naomi's sons marry Moabite girls — but soon after, Naomi's husband and sons die. Ruth (one of Naomi's daughters-in-law) stays very loyal to her Israelite mother-in-law, and becomes devoted to God. This bloodline eventually produces King David. The message is, Good things happen to those who are nice to people from other lands.

"Male and female he created them" — Genesis 1:27 NIV

1) The above passage is sometimes read as meaning that men and women are seen as equals before God, although different, and with different responsibilities. (God did create two different sexes after all, so he can't have wanted us all to be identical.)
2) Some people involved with the feminist movement (fighting for women's rights) argue that the expectation for women to become wives and mothers is unfair, and has hindered women's progress.
3) Judaism doesn't suggest that women should not be able to follow their chosen career. However, there is still a belief that motherhood is a privilege, and women should devote some of their life to it.
4) But there are definitely differences of opinion on this. Orthodox Jews aim to uphold many of the ancient Jewish traditions, and so would be more likely to suggest that women should remain at home as mothers and wives.
5) However, Reform Jews are willing to interpret traditional teachings so that they are, perhaps, more relevant to the modern age. For this reason they're less strict when it comes to the roles of men and women.

There are also rules governing SYNAGOGUE WORSHIP. Usually ten men (called a minyan) are required for a service, and it is men who read from the Torah. Also, men and women in Orthodox synagogues have separate areas for prayer.
Reform Jews don't accept all these rules, however — women can form a minyan, and even become rabbis.

I don't believe the Jonah story — it all sounds a bit fishy...

Jews have suffered from a great deal of racism and persecution over the years. By far the most extreme form of social injustice was the Holocaust in World War II, when discrimination became government policy. It serves as a reminder to everyone of how much suffering can arise from racial hatred.

Religious Help for Immigrants

Christianity, Islam & Judaism

Hundreds of thousands of people move to the UK every year — either looking for work or to find refuge from persecution (asylum seekers). And there are plenty of religious organisations out there to help them...

Immigrants Often Face Difficulties

1) Many immigrants arrive with either no, or very poor, English — so they need interpreters while they learn the language.
2) They're often unfamiliar with British customs and laws, so can find themselves in trouble without understanding why.
3) Many asylum seekers have suffered physical, mental, emotional or sexual abuses in their countries, which can leave them seriously traumatised.
4) Without good English and an understanding of the system, it can be very difficult to get good-quality legal advice, register for healthcare or find accommodation.
5) Immigrants are frequently exploited as unofficial, cheap labour, paid well below the minimum wage.
6) Some people accuse immigrants of taking homes and jobs from local people. This attitude can lead to discrimination and abuse (ranging from playground name-calling to physical attacks).

Religious Organisations Offer Practical Help

Christianity, Islam and Judaism agree that all human beings should be treated fairly and humanely. So there are organisations from all three faiths working to improve the lot of immigrants to this country. You need to know some examples of these religious organisations and the work they do:

The Boaz Trust

A Christian charity based in Manchester, set up to help asylum seekers whose initial application to stay in the UK has been turned down. Many of these people aren't allowed to work and get no help from the Government, so they're entirely dependent on charity for food, accommodation and any legal help they might need for an appeal.

The Jesuit Refugee Service

An international Roman Catholic organisation, with bases in over 50 countries worldwide. JRS offers pastoral services (taking care of people's spiritual well-being), counselling, English-language teaching and help with healthcare and legal representation. They also campaign across Europe against the detention of asylum seekers. (Detention means holding asylum seekers in a centre while deciding if they should be allowed into the community or sent back to where they came from.)

Islamic Aid

An international Muslim organisation dedicated to reducing poverty and deprivation. Their work in the UK centres on improving the lives of Muslim immigrants, e.g. by raising awareness of the problem of 'ghettos' and tackling unemployment among UK Muslims.

The Jewish Council for Racial Equality (JCORE)

A Jewish organisation, based in the UK. They campaign for the rights of asylum seekers, raise awareness of the problems faced by immigrants and offer all sorts of practical help. For example, they have a 'refugee doctors project' that gives information and practical help to trained immigrant doctors, to help them re-train to practise in the UK.

Bienvenue, Willkommen, Witajcie, Swaagatam, Huan yin...

There are tens of thousands of failed asylum seekers in the UK, living off the charity of organisations like Boaz and JCORE. They have no home, no legal way of making money, no access to medicine or education for their children — it's a terrible way to live. But as far as the law's concerned, they have no right to be here at all...

General

The UK as a Multi-Faith Society

All through history, people from different cultures have come to settle in Britain, bringing with them their own beliefs and customs. It makes our society rich and diverse, but can sometimes cause problems.

The UK is a Diverse, Multi-Faith Society

1) The United Kingdom is a diverse, multi-faith society — there are a wide range of Christian denominations, and in England and Wales almost 9% of the population say they follow a non-Christian religion.
2) In most major towns and cities you'll find a variety of places of worship — including different churches, synagogues and mosques.
3) Children in UK schools are taught about all major world faiths in an attempt to increase understanding and tolerance.

Although some Roman Catholic and other church schools limit the amount of time spent looking at other religions.

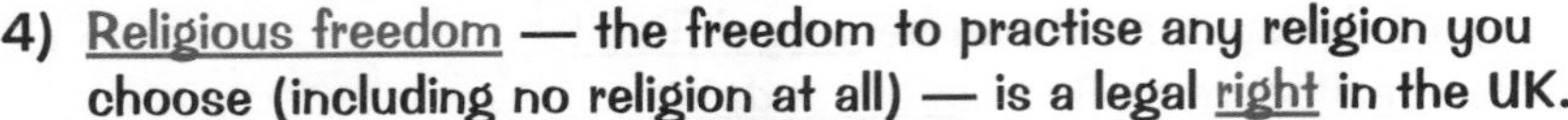

4) Religious freedom — the freedom to practise any religion you choose (including no religion at all) — is a legal right in the UK.
5) The religious diversity of the UK provides a great opportunity for increasing understanding, and for finding common ground between the different faiths.
6) But that isn't the only advantage of a multi-faith society. Along with their faiths, these different cultural groups bring their customs, dress, art, music, food, architecture...
7) All this helps to make the UK a really vibrant and interesting place to live.

Conversion and Interfaith Marriages are Issues in the UK

But along with religious diversity and freedom come the issues of conversion and interfaith marriages.

CONVERSION

In the past, Christians often believed they had the right to make people take up their faith. In general, Christians are much more tolerant now, but evangelical Christians still consider it a priority to 'win people for Christ'. This is because they don't believe that a person can get to Heaven any other way (see next page).

Muslims are happy to accept converts, but they don't usually go out trying to convert people. However, rejecting Islam to take another faith (apostasy) is a sin that's still punishable by death.

While the early Jews accepted converts to the faith, modern Orthodox Jews aren't very keen to at all. Reform Jews will accept converts after a period of study (usually about 18 months) but they don't encourage conversion either.

INTERFAITH MARRIAGES

As a rule, interfaith marriages are disapproved of — unless either the husband or the wife intends to convert at some point.

Children of a mixed marriage are much less likely to be brought up as observant members of either religion (although the child of a Muslim is considered a Muslim, and the child of a Jewish mother is considered Jewish — whatever the faith of the other parent). And it can be difficult for any member of the family to really stay a part of their own faith community. There are groups like the 'Inter-Faith Marriage Network' that offer advice and support for mixed-faith couples.

Pluralists say there's Room for Everyone

1) Most religious believers are happy to live alongside other faiths in the UK. Organisations representing every major faith in the UK belong to the 'Inter Faith Network for the UK'.
2) The aim of this network is to promote mutual understanding, combat prejudice and help build community cohesion.
3) This is an example of religious pluralism — the idea that every faith has as much right to exist as any other, and that there's room for everyone.

The Inter Faith Network for the UK describes itself as based "...on the principle that dialogue and cooperation can only prosper if they are rooted in respectful relationships which do not blur or undermine the distinctiveness of different religious traditions".

Pluralism — is that, like, being against more than one of something...

Christianity, Judaism and Islam have a lot in common — which comes as a shock to some people. But don't go getting the idea that these are the only three religions in the world. If you want to do another RS Exam after this one, there'll be plenty of other stuff to learn about. Hurrah! ... ... I said HURRAH! ... oh...

Attitudes to Other Religions

Christianity, Islam & Judaism

Christianity, Islam and Judaism have a great deal in common, and their approach to other religions is generally one of tolerance and mutual understanding. Over the years, though, there have been times of misunderstanding, ignorance and intolerance, which have led to discrimination and war (e.g. the Crusades).

Christianity Teaches that Jesus is the Only Path to God

"I am the way and the truth and the life. No one comes to the Father except through me." John 14:6 NIV

1) Christians generally believe that people have the right to practise any faith, although they might argue that only Christianity has the truth about God. This passage stresses the Christian belief that it's only through following the teachings of Jesus Christ that people can reach God.
2) In the Decree "Ad Gentes", the Roman Catholic Church makes it clear that "...the Church still has the obligation and also the sacred right to evangelise all men". 'Evangelise' means spread the Christian message with the aim of converting people (see previous page).
3) This approach could be described as exclusive — it doesn't particularly welcome other faiths, and may even reject them because Christianity is seen as the only way.
4) But not all Christians accept this. Christian inclusivists believe that there's at least some truth in what other religions say about God.

Muslims believe Islam is the Only True Faith

1) Muslims believe that Islam is the only true faith — although there is an acceptance that all righteous people will be favoured by Allah, as he knows all we do.
2) Muslims believe that men like Adam, Ibrahim (Abraham), Musa (Moses) and Isa (Jesus) were all Prophets of Allah. So the Torah and the Bible are also holy scriptures revealed by Allah (albeit edited from their original form). This suggests that Islam is an inclusive faith.
3) But some Muslims interpret the scriptures to argue that Islam should be exclusive, and shouldn't have anything to do with other faiths. And like Christians, some Muslims feel they have a mission to lead non-Muslims to Allah.
4) However, many Muslims in the UK live side by side with other religious believers, and some take part in interfaith groups (see previous page).

"Indeed, those who believed and those who were Jews or Christians... those [among them] who believed in Allah and the Last Day and did righteousness — will have their reward with their Lord..." Qur'an 2:62

E.g. The Centre for the Study of Islam and Christian-Muslim Relations.

Jews believe Judaism is the Only True Faith (for Jews)

1) Judaism teaches that it is the only true faith for Jews to follow, but is tolerant of other faiths.
2) Most faiths have similar moral and spiritual laws and so are tolerated by Judaism. Because of this, there's no real desire to convert people.
3) People of any religion are generally deemed to be righteous if they follow the Noachide Code — moral laws given to Noah after the flood that prohibit idolatry, murder, theft, sexual immorality and blasphemy.

...and that whole tearing the flesh from a still-living animal and eating it thing — that's right out.*
Aww... you're joking?
Baaa!!

4) Islam and Judaism have very similar beliefs in one all-powerful God. However, some Jews have difficulties with the Christian belief that Jesus Christ was the incarnation of God. And with the use of statues and icons in Roman Catholic and Orthodox Christianity, which they see as idolatry.
5) But there's still a great deal of mutual respect, and Jewish participation in interfaith groups is common. One example of an interfaith group in the UK is 'The Council of Christians and Jews'.

I know what you're thinking — this is a righteous page...

So exclusivists believe that their religion is the only way to salvation. Inclusivists believe that other religions have some truth in them. And pluralists believe that all religions are equally valid. And there are followers of all three philosophies in the three main religions. Ooh, it's a tricky subject, is this... make no mistake.

* Noachide Law No. 6 — mmm... lovely

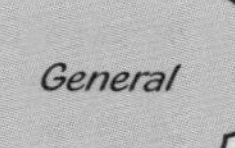

The Media: Religion and Society

Community cohesion isn't really much of a story until everything goes pear-shaped. But when it does, it gets everyone's attention.

The Media Raises Sensitive Issues

For new entrants to the UK, life in a new country isn't easy (see page 33). The media has to strike a balance — drawing attention to problems and issues that may be of public concern, but without encouraging racism or xenophobia (fear or hatred of people from other countries).

Immigration is Regularly in the News

The mainstream British press would deny that it ever carries a racist or discriminatory message, but some people argue that it encourages prejudice.

1) Elements of the British media have described immigration as a big problem and have called for stricter controls on who's allowed to settle in the country.
2) They point to the strain placed on social services, the competition for jobs and the fact that immigrants often send a large proportion of the money they earn back to their country of origin.
3) Some think this media attention has made life harder for migrants, by turning people against them, and ignores the positive impact they have — creating economic activity often in deprived areas.

Asylum Seekers Often Hit the Headlines

1) Some British newspapers have been very critical of government policy on asylum, particularly when failed asylum seekers have remained in the country, or committed crimes.
2) Campaigners claim that these reports lead to discrimination against those trying to escape persecution. The newspapers argue that they're just highlighting flaws in and abuses of the system.

Rioting in 2001 Highlighted Tensions

1) In 2001, activity by the far-right group, the National Front, sparked off rioting in Oldham and Burnley. This unrest spread to Bradford, a city that had seen decades of high immigration, which had developed a number of ethnically segregated neighbourhoods.
2) Much of the violence was focused in Manningham, a mainly Pakistani area of the city, where it was reported that around one thousand Asian youths confronted riot police.
3) News reports featured local religious leaders — including the Archbishop of Bradford and members of local Muslim organisations — expressing their distress and appealing for calm.
4) In the aftermath, the leaders of Bradford's different religious groups met up with the Home Secretary to try to end the mistrust between their communities.
5) While some in the media applauded the role played by religious organisations, others complained that focusing on religion took attention away from the problem of racism, and the real social and economic difficulties faced by the people of Bradford.

In 2006 Channel 4 made Bradford Riots, a drama which tells the story of Karim, a Muslim student from Bradford, who gets caught up in the rioting and ends up being given a harsh prison sentence.

- Religion plays an important, but background role in the film. The Imam in the mosque offers spiritual guidance rather than practical advice.
- Religion is seen as an inescapable part of the characters' identities — but one that they are sometimes reduced to. At the end, Karim's cellmate calls him simply 'Muslim-boy'.
- The film reflects on the uncertainty and vulnerability felt by Britain's Muslim communities in the wake of the 9/11 terrorist attacks.

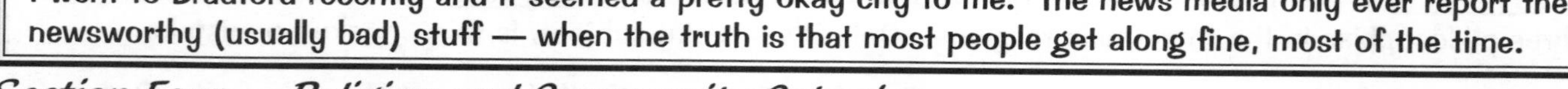

For more on this — keep your eye on the papers...

I went to Bradford recently and it seemed a pretty okay city to me. The news media only ever report the newsworthy (usually bad) stuff — when the truth is that most people get along fine, most of the time.

Practice Questions

Can't we all just learn to get along? Well, no — you have to learn all the stuff in this section first. This covers some pretty big issues — prejudice, discrimination, tolerance... and it's your job to pick your way through this muddle that we call twenty-first century society.

Shall we begin...?

1) What is:
   a) discrimination?
   b) prejudice?
   c) racism?
   d) sexism?
   e) an ethnic minority?
   f) community cohesion?
   g) racial harmony?
   h) a multi-ethnic society?
   i) religious freedom?
   j) religious pluralism?

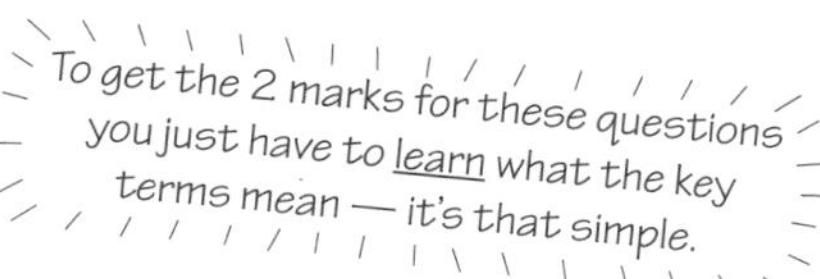

To get the 2 marks for these questions
you just have to learn what the key
terms mean — it's that simple.

2) For each of the following questions, give two reasons for your point of view.
   a) Do you think religions tend to create conflict in mixed communities?
   b) Do you think Christianity is fair to women?
   c) Do you think different religions should have the right to try and convert people in the UK?
   d) Do you think that people with religious faith should ever consider a mixed marriage?

Remember, you're not getting marks here for having the 'right' opinion — only for having the reasons to back it up. Each of these questions is worth 4 marks in the exam.

3) For these questions, you need to express yourself as clearly as possible — make sure your writing is correct, accurate and well organised.
   a) Explain how the British Government has sought to combat discrimination and improve community cohesion in recent decades.
   b) Choose one religion and explain its teachings on gender equality in religious matters.
   c) Explain how one religion's teachings encourage racial harmony.
   d) Explain the difficulties faced by immigrants to the UK and how one religious organisation works to help them.
   e) Choose one religion and explain its teachings on other faiths.

These are the big 8-mark ones — so they're worth taking a little bit of time over. And don't forget, you're also being assessed on how well you write.

4) Read the following statements:
   a) "Truly religious people could never be racist."
   b) "The media tends to promote conflict more than cohesion in mixed ethnic communities."
   c) "Religion encourages discrimination against women."
   d) "No religion that believes it is the world's one true faith will ever really support community cohesion."

   For each statement:

   (i) Do you agree? Give reasons for your opinion.

   (ii) Give reasons why some people may disagree with you.

   In your answers you should refer to at least one religion.

This lot of questions should remind you that you need to learn both sides of the big arguments — no matter how passionately you believe in your own opinion. 3 marks for your opinion — 3 marks for someone else's.

General

Do Well in Your Exam

You've learnt all the facts — now it's time to get those grades.

You'll have a 1½ Hour Exam on Religion and Life

1) For the Religion and Life exam you'll have to answer a question on each of the four topics — Believing in God or Allah or the Almighty (depending on which unit you're studying), Matters of Life and Death, Marriage and the Family, and Religion and Community Cohesion.
2) For each topic you'll have the choice of two questions. Each question is worth 20 marks and will be split into four parts. You have to answer all four parts of each question you choose.
3) Your answer for Section 1, Believing in God or Allah or the Almighty, will be assessed for spelling, punctuation and grammar (see p.41-44). There are 4 extra marks available, so make your writing as accurate as you can.
4) For part (c) of each question you'll be marked on the quality of your English — see p.39 for more on this.

There are Easy Marks for knowing what things Mean

Two marks out of each question are for just knowing what the important words mean. These questions don't carry a lot of marks, so keep your answers short and to the point — but make sure you define the word properly. Learn the terms that relate to your unit from the glossary.

a) What is meant by **natural evil**? (2 marks)

The evil and suffering which is not caused by people, but by the world itself.

Try to answer this kind of question in one sentence.

This is too long. You don't have time to write an essay on questions that don't offer many marks. Keep your answer short and to the point.

Evil is that which brings suffering into the world. Natural evil is the term which defines the evil which is not moral evil. Moral evil is that evil which is created by humans: it is man-made evil. Natural evil, in contrast, is that evil which is not man-made, but 'natural': events such as earthquakes, floods and storms can bring suffering and are hence natural evils.

But this is just an example, not a definition, so it'd only get you 1 mark.

Things like earthquakes and floods.

You'll be asked about What you Think

There's no right answer to this kind of question — only good answers that'll get you lots of marks and bad answers that won't. The difference between the two is that good answers give clearly developed reasons. You can make reference to the religious teachings you have studied, but in part (b) you don't have to.

b) Do you agree with the UK ban on euthanasia in all circumstances?
Give two reasons for your point of view. (4 marks)

I don't believe that euthanasia is wrong in all circumstances because in cases where people have no quality of life, forcing them to continue living is just forcing them to suffer.

As a Christian I believe that we have a duty to help those who are suffering. In some cases, helping them end their suffering may be the best we can do.

Both of these answers are pretty good despite arguing different things from different perspectives.

Make sure you back up each point with a relevant reason.

As a Muslim I believe that euthanasia is wrong in all circumstances because suffering is a test of our faith, and those who remain faithful will be rewarded after death.

Doctors and nurses have a duty to protect life, and to never harm their patients. They do not have the authority to decide when it is right for their patients to die.

Try to use proper sentences. You won't get extra marks for it on this question — but it'll make it easier for the person marking your paper.

Are exams a moral or a natural evil?

Don't forget — you don't get marks for what you believe, only for the reasons you give to back up your opinions. So make sure you know all the main arguments, for all the big topics.

Do Well in Your Exam

General

More stuff for you on the exam right here. Get stuck in.

You'll have to Explain Why...

1) For the part (c) question, you'll get some marks for the quality of your written English. This includes structuring your answer, using a formal style and having correct grammar and punctuation.
2) You'll also get marks for using the kind of fancy words that you'll find in the glossary — learn what they mean, how to use them, and how to spell them.

Best break out the best handwriting for this one.

c) Explain why the followers of one religion should help the poor.	(8 marks)

You'd only use Judaism as an example if you'd studied it during the course.

Jewish people follow the teaching of the Torah which says that there is a responsibility to help those who have fallen on hard times and are unable to support themselves.

It says in the book of Deuteronomy that people should not be "hardhearted or tightfisted" towards the poor.

Not only are Jewish people encouraged by their teachings to help the poor, they have an obligation to carry out a ritual gift to the poor in the form of the tzedakah. This requires followers to give a proportion of their income away. It is so important that even poor people are obliged to fulfil the obligation.

It won't hurt if you remember a little bit of scripture.

You'll get marks for using 'specialist vocabulary' — i.e. words like tzedakah.

3) If you structure your answer well you'll get more marks — so sketch out a plan before you write out your answer.
4) The best marks will go to those who put in a number of reasons and/or develop their reasons well.
5) To get top marks you usually have to give either 'four brief reasons, three reasons with one developed, two developed reasons or a comprehensive explanation using one reason only'. So if you've only got one point to make in an answer like this, you'd better make sure you know it inside out. (The answer above gives two developed reasons.)

c) Explain why the followers of one religion should promote religious tolerance.	(8 marks)

It says in the Qur'an that Allah created everyone from a single soul so that we could "know each other", not so we could "despise each other." This suggests that there is a requirement for Muslims to be friendly to other faiths.

Muslims believe that Islam is the only true faith, and as such they may feel a responsibility to convert non-Muslims. However the Qur'an states that those who follow other religions faithfully, especially Judaism and Christianity, shall be rewarded in the next life. This suggests that Muslims should respect people of other faiths.

Perhaps the most important reason why Muslims should want to live in harmony with Christians and Jews is the fact that they believe that they all worship the same God.

You'd only use Islam as an example if you'd studied it during the course.

It can be good to put your best point last.

Thou shalt write clearly...

As much as you may know every little fact that pops up in this book, a large chunk of how well you do in exams will come down to, well..., how good you are at exams. Make sure you spend enough time reading through these pages, and enough time practising doing exam-style questions under timed conditions. It'll all pay off in the end.

General

Do Well in Your Exam

Here's a page on those pesky questions where you have to understand other people's opinions.

You need to know Both Sides of the Argument

1) In part (d) you'll get the same marks for writing what you think and for writing what people who disagree with you think. So spend the same time and effort on each.
2) You'll be told to refer to a religion here, so make sure you do. If you don't do this in at least one part of your answer, you can only score a maximum of half marks.

> d) "Scientific advances make the existence of God less likely."
> In your answers you should refer to at least one religion.
> (i) Do you agree? Give reasons for your opinion. (3 marks)
> (ii) Give reasons why some people may disagree with you. (3 marks)

If you're studying the Christianity, Islam or Judaism units you'll be asked to refer specifically to the religion you're studying.

(i) I do not believe that scientific discoveries prove that there is no God. I would argue that the scriptures, which scientific discoveries have made it difficult to believe in literally, should be interpreted symbolically.

I would argue that the scientific explanation of creation is not a problem for those who believe in God, only for those who believe in the literal truth of the scriptures. Just because the universe was not created as described in the Bible does not mean that God was not involved.

Although science can explain more and more about events in the natural world, I would argue that belief in God does not need those things, and that faith is based on inward things, like numinous experiences, rather than on external evidence.

(ii) People who believe that science has made the existence of God less likely, would argue that one of the most important proofs of God has been disproved. The argument from design — that the world is so complex it had to have a designer — could be said to have been disproved by the theory of evolution which shows how complexity could have arisen without being externally guided.

Some people would argue that the Big Bang theory proves that God did not create the world, and that questions about what was before the universe do not even make sense. They would argue that this removes the need to believe in God as a 'first cause'.

Try to make the reasons why people disagree with you as good as the reasons for your own opinion.

(i) I believe that scientific theories do mean we should accept the existence of God is less likely. People used to believe based on the fact that they thought God had designed and created the world as described in their scriptures. As science has come up with theories that explain these things without the need for a god, we should accept that the existence of God is less likely. Although science can neither prove nor disprove the existence of God, it has undermined some of the key evidence for God.

(ii) Some would argue that scientific advances do not make God's existence less likely, as some people at the very forefront of scientific advance, have continued to find the universe evidence enough for religious faith. Albert Einstein said: "When I see all the glories of the cosmos, I can't help but believe that there is a divine hand behind it all." This shows that some people would suggest that the amazing things science discovers can be considered as suggesting there is a god.

This answer will lose marks because it doesn't refer to a specific religion in either part.

Don't waffle. If you keep your answer more to the point, you'll get more in. And that means more marks.

If you can only think of one reason in the exam, make sure you develop it as best you can.

Don't forget the Basics

1) Read the questions carefully. Make sure you read both questions on each topic before you pick one of them. Remember, you've got to answer all the parts of the questions you pick.
2) Be aware of how much time you're using. Try to leave a bit of time at the end to check your answers.

"I think exams are rubbish" — "I think exams are great..."

...but that's just because they pay me to put revision guides together. Make sure you learn the different arguments for both sides of the key issues. It's not a bad lesson to take away from the exam — even if you believe something strongly, it's worthwhile knowing why other people don't. You might even change your mind...

Spelling, Punctuation and Grammar

General

You get marks in your exams for having good SPaG (Spelling, Punctuation and Grammar). This stuff might not be particularly thrilling but if you can get it right, it's easy marks. This page is about checking your work...

Remember to Check what you've Written

1) Leave 5 minutes at the end of the exam to check your work.
2) 5 minutes isn't long, so there won't be time to check everything thoroughly. Look for the most obvious spelling, punctuation and grammar mistakes.
3) Start by checking your answer to Section 1, Believing in God or Allah or the Almighty, because it carries SPaG marks. Only check the rest of your answers if you've got time.

Check for common Spelling Mistakes

When you're writing under pressure, it's easy to let spelling mistakes creep in, but there are a few things you can watch out for:

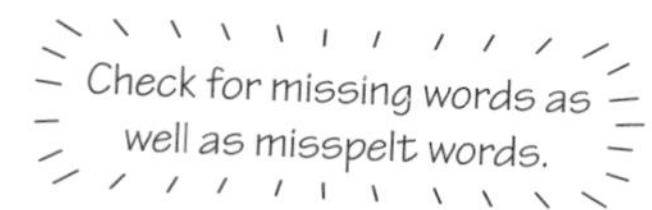

Check for missing words as well as misspelt words.

1) Look out for words which sound the same but mean different things and are spelt differently. Make sure you've used the correct one. For example, 'their', 'there' and 'they're':

Suffering may lead some people to question their belief in God.

There are many reasons why people believe in life after death.

Jews condemn unfairness, and they're expected to help the poor by giving money to charity.

2) Don't use text speak, and always write words out in full. For example, use 'and' instead of '&' or '+'. Don't use 'etc.' when you could give more examples or a better explanation.
3) Make sure you've used the appropriate technical terms (like 'euthanasia', 'sacrament' or 'Shari'ah'). If they're spelt correctly it'll really impress the examiner.

Make sure your Grammar and Punctuation are Correct

1) Check you've used capital letters, full stops and question marks correctly (see p.44).
2) Make sure your writing isn't too chatty and doesn't use slang words. It should be formal.
3) Watch out for sentences where your writing switches between different tenses. You should usually stick to one tense throughout your answer (don't worry if you've used a quote that's in a different tense though).
4) Check that you've started a new paragraph every time you make a new point. It's important that your answer isn't just one long block of text (see p.44).
5) Watch out for tricksy little grammar mistakes:
   - Remember — 'it's' (with an apostrophe) is short for 'it is' or 'it has'. 'Its' (without an apostrophe) means 'belonging to it'.
   - It's always 'should have', not 'should of' (the same goes for 'could have' and 'would have' too).

   If you know that you often confuse two words, like 'it's' and 'its', watch out for them when you're checking your work in the exam.

Check, check, check, goose, check, check, check...

Blimey, there's a lot of stuff to check... which is why it's really important to practise it all before the exam. That way it'll be second nature, so you'll do it all automatically and make fewer errors in the first place.

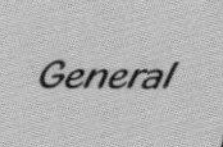

Spelling, Punctuation and Grammar

Making a mistake in your exam is not the end of the world, so don't panic if you do find one. If you just cross it out neatly and correct the mistake, you won't lose any marks at all — excellent.

Make your corrections Neatly

1) If the mistake is just one word or a short phrase, cross it out neatly and write the correct word above it.

> A stable family can give a child a sense of identity and a feeling of security, teaching him or her how to behave in different social situations and how to give and ~~recieve~~ receive love.

If only someone had told Graham about the double strike.

2) If you've forgotten to start a new paragraph, use a double strike (like this '//') to show where the new paragraph should begin:

See p.44 for more on paragraphs.

> The Third Pillar of Islam commands that Muslims, no matter how rich or poor they are, give 2.5% of their yearly savings to charity. // Christians feel it is their duty to be charitable. There are a number of Christian charities that help the needy in the UK and around the world, for example Christian Aid and CAFOD.

Use an Asterisk to add Extra Information

1) If you've missed something out, think about whether you have space to write the missing bit above the line you've already written. If you can, use a '^' to show exactly where it should go.

> Contraception is anything that prevents a woman becoming pregnant. It can be temporary (e.g. condoms) or permanent (e.g. sterilisation). Traditionally, the Roman Catholic Church has disagreed with the use of contraception. However, many individual Roman Catholics support ^the use of contraception, particularly because it can help to prevent the spread of diseases such as AIDS.

2) If the bit you've missed out won't fit above the line, use an asterisk (like this '*') to show the examiner where the missing bit should go.
3) Write the missing words at the end of your answer with another asterisk next to them.

> Racism is prejudice against someone from a different cultural or religious background.* It is often a result of ignorance, misunderstanding or segregation.
>
> * or someone with a different skin colour.

Cross Out anything you Don't want to be Marked

1) If you've written something that you don't want the examiner to mark, cross it out neatly.
2) Cross out any notes. But if you don't finish your answer in time, don't cross out your plan — the examiner might look at it to see what you were going to write.
3) Don't scribble things out without thinking — it'll make your answers look messy.

When making corrections, neatness is the name of ^the game

Examiners love it if your answer is neat and tidy — it makes it super easy for them to read. This means they can spend more time giving you lots of marks for the great stuff you've written. So neatness is win-win.

Spelling, Punctuation and Grammar

General

Some words are darn tricky to spell. The only way to be sure you'll get them right is to learn them off by heart. This page has some of the most common ones you'll need to know for your RS exams.

Learn these Useful Words

The underlined words are useful in a lot of answers, so you need to know how to spell them.

There are complicated arguments for and against abortion.

Suicide is when someone takes their own life, usually because they are depressed.

There are definite differences in opinion between Orthodox Jews and Reform Jews.

Most Muslims believe it's unwise for young men and women to mix freely.

Not all religious believers agree about whether divorce should be allowed.

Basically, Islam, Christianity and Judaism all think that marriage is the correct context for sexual activity.

Racial segregation is when people of different races do their daily activities separately.

Spell Technical Words Correctly

There are a lot of technical words in RS. You need to be able to spell them correctly.
Learn these examples to start you off. The coloured letters are the tricky bits to watch out for.

conscience
euthanasia
celibacy
sacrament
immoral
omnipotent
promiscuity
prejudice
atheism
agnosticism
asylum
adultery
resurrection
justice
agnosticism
omniscient
immigration
procreation
reconciliation
suicide

Make sure you know the specific technical words for your topics. For example, if you're studying the Islamic view on marriage, you would need to know words like 'mahr' (a dowry) and 'nikah' (the Muslim marriage contract). There's a list of technical terms in the glossary on p.45-46.

You might think revision is immoral — you'd be wrong...

You could always try to make up rhymes to remember how to spell key words. For example, for 'conscience' you could have 'Mrs C, Mrs O, Mrs N S C, Mrs I, Mrs E, Mrs N C E'. Hmm, well it's a work in progress...

General

Spelling, Punctuation and Grammar

This page is full of tips for good punctuation and grammar to help you avoid making any silly mistakes, hurrah!

You need to Punctuate Properly...

1) **Always use a capital letter at the start of a sentence.**
   Use capital letters for names of particular people, places and things. For example:

   Many Jews live in Israel, where the official language is Hebrew.

   All sentences start with capital letters. — The name of a group of religious believers. — A country. — The name of a language.

2) **Full stops go at the end of sentences, e.g. 'Muslims worship Allah.'**
   Question marks go at the end of questions, e.g. 'What is divorce?'
3) **Use commas when you use more than one adjective to describe something or to separate items in a list:**

   In a diverse, multi-faith city you are likely to find a variety of places of worship, including mosques, churches, synagogues and Hindu temples.

4) **Commas can also join two points into one sentence with a joining word (such as 'and', 'or', 'so' or 'but'):**

   Muslims are happy to accept converts, but they don't usually try to convert people themselves.

   Muslims feel that it's the right of both husband and wife to try for children, so both partners must agree to any contraception.

5) **Commas can also be used to separate extra information in a sentence:**

   The Jewish marriage ceremony takes place beneath a wedding canopy, a piece of cloth supported by four poles, called a chuppah.

   One of the best-known religious TV programmes is Songs of Praise, which features the singing of Christian hymns.

   When you use commas like this, the sentence should still make sense when the extra bit is taken out.

...and use Grammar Correctly

1) **Don't change tenses in your writing by mistake:**

   Some schools of Islam allow abortion before 120 days if there is a good reason for it.

   This sentence is correct because the verbs are both in the present tense. Writing 'was' instead of 'is' would be wrong.

2) **Don't use double negatives. You should only use a negative once in a sentence:**

   Don't put 'nothing' here.

   Some Muslims argue that Islam should be exclusive and should not have anything to do with other faiths.

3) **Write your longer answers in paragraphs. A paragraph is a group of sentences which talk about the same thing or follow on from each other. You need to start a new paragraph when you start making a new point. You show a new paragraph by starting a new line and leaving a gap (an indent) before you start writing:**

   This gap shows a new paragraph.

   Jews believe that Judaism is the only true faith, but they don't try to convert non-Jews. Many faiths have similar moral and spiritual laws, so Jews are tolerant of them.

   In many ways, the beliefs of Jews, Christians and Muslims are very similar. They have similar principles and ideas about the way that believers should live their lives...

   When you plan long answers, remember that you should write a new paragraph for each of your main points.

Phew, now you're fully SPaG-ed and ready to go...

Having good SPaG is a great way to get marks in RS exams, and having bad SPaG is a great way to lose marks. Which is why it's dead important to learn all the stuff on this page (and all the other pages too).

Glossary

Everyone needs the blue definitions. The green ones are for Islam only. The purple ones are for Judaism only.

abortion	Removing a foetus from the womb before it is able to survive, ending the pregnancy.
adultery	A married person having sex with someone who isn't their husband or wife. It can also be used more generally to mean cheating on your partner, whether you're married or not.
agnosticism	A belief that it's impossible to know whether or not there's a god. Not knowing if God exists.
akhirah (Islam)	The concept of life after death. This is a key Islamic belief.
al'Jannah (Islam)	The afterlife paradise — described as 'gardens of delight' in the Qur'an.
assisted suicide	Ending your own life with the help of someone else. For example, a terminally ill patient asking their doctor for a fatal dose of pills.
atheism	A complete denial of the existence of a god.
barzakh (Islam)	The "cold sleep" that the soul enters after death while it waits for the Day of Judgement.
civil partnership	The joining of a same-sex couple with the same rights and responsibilities as in a civil marriage. Civil partnerships came into effect in the UK in 2005.
cohabitation	Living together in a sexual relationship without being married.
community cohesion	The bonds holding a community together, e.g. shared values, shared culture.
contraception	Anything that aims to prevent a woman becoming pregnant.
contract (Islam)	The marriage contract (or nikah) is a formal agreement that both the bride and groom have to consent to before they're married. Both parties can add conditions to the contract.
conversion	When someone's life is first changed by becoming a follower of a faith.
discrimination	Treating different people, or groups of people, differently (usually unfairly).
ethnic minority	A group of people who have a different ethnic background from most of the population.
euthanasia	Ending someone's life to relieve their suffering, especially from an incurable, painful illness.
faithfulness	Staying loyal. In the context of a marriage, this usually means staying sexually loyal.
free will	The ability to choose how to behave. All three religions believe humans have free will.
homosexuality	Being attracted to members of the same sex.
immortality of the soul	The belief that the soul of a person lives on after the death of the body — either being reincarnated on earth, or moving to a different kind of existence.
interfaith marriages	Marriages in which the bride and groom follow different faiths.
ketubah (Judaism)	The marriage contract, which sets out the couple's rights and responsibilities. The traditional text dates back to the 2nd century BCE.
kiddushin (Judaism)	Betrothal — the first part of the marriage ceremony. The word comes from a root meaning 'sanctified' or 'holy'.
mahr (Islam)	A dowry paid by a groom to the bride when they get married. This dowry remains the property of the wife in the event of a divorce.
miracle	An event believed to be the work of God, that can't be explained by the laws of science.
moral evil	Suffering caused by human beings, e.g. war, murder, rape, torture.
multi-ethnic society	A society with members from several different national or cultural backgrounds.
multi-faith society	A society with members from several different faiths (it's not exactly rocket science).

Glossary

natural evil	Suffering caused by the world we live in, e.g. disease, floods, earthquakes, hurricanes.
near-death experience	A vision experienced by someone close to death, usually an 'out-of-body' experience. While apparently physically dead, the person glimpses what they believe to be an afterlife.
non-voluntary euthanasia	When a patient is unable to ask for euthanasia, the decision is made by someone else — usually doctors and family members (compare with voluntary euthanasia).
nuclear family	A family made up of a mother, a father and their children living together.
numinous	An experience that inspires awe and wonder, in which someone can feel God's presence.
omni-benevolent	Showing unlimited love and compassion.
omnipotent	Having unlimited powers — all things are possible.
omniscient	Knowing everything — in the past, present and future.
Orthodox Jews (Judaism)	Orthodox means 'right belief'. Orthodox Jews live strictly by the Torah and feel that traditional Jewish beliefs and practices should be kept to.
paranormal	Things that science can't explain, which are thought to have spiritual causes, e.g. ghosts.
prayer	An attempt to contact God directly, often in the form of a conversation.
prejudice	Judging something or someone with no good reason, or without full knowledge of a situation.
pre-marital sex	Sex before marriage. All three religions disapprove of it, Islam very strongly.
procreation	Having children.
promiscuity	Having many sexual partners.
quality of life	The idea that the well-being of a person, including how well they can deal with the everyday tasks of living, makes a difference to whether life is worth living. In medical ethics, a poor quality of life is often used as an argument in favour of euthanasia (compare with sanctity of life).
racial harmony	People of different races living and working together in peace.
racism	Discrimination against people of other races — often based on unfair stereotypes.
re-constituted family	A family in which at least one of the adults has children from a previous relationship.
Reform Jews (Judaism)	Reform Judaism began at the end of the 18th century. Reform Jews don't view the Torah as the direct word of God, but rather as people's interpretations of it. As such, only the moral laws are seen as binding — the ritual laws are open to reinterpretation in response to changes in society.
reincarnation	The rebirth of a soul in a new body after death.
religious freedom	The freedom of a person or community to openly practise and teach their religion, to change religion or to not follow a religion at all. Many societies consider this a fundamental human right.
religious pluralism	Accepting that more than one religious viewpoint is valid, and that every faith has as much right to exist as any other. (Ooooh, philosophy.)
re-marriage	Marrying again after being divorced.
resurrection	Being brought back to life after death. This could be the resurrection of the body or the soul.
sanctity of life	A belief that all human life is sacred, or holy. In medical ethics, the 'sanctity of life' argument states that we don't have the right to choose when a life ends (compare with quality of life).
sexism	Discrimination based on someone's gender (male or female).
voluntary euthanasia	When an ill person actively requests assistance to die, or asks doctors to remove a treatment that's keeping them alive (compare with non-voluntary euthanasia).

Index

Index